Conversations with
LeAnne Howe

Literary Conversations Series
Monika Gehlawat
General Editor

Conversations with LeAnne Howe

Edited by Kirstin L. Squint

University Press of Mississippi / Jackson

The University Press of Mississippi is the scholarly publishing agency of the Mississippi Institutions of Higher Learning: Alcorn State University, Delta State University, Jackson State University, Mississippi State University, Mississippi University for Women, Mississippi Valley State University, University of Mississippi, and University of Southern Mississippi.

www.upress.state.ms.us

The University Press of Mississippi is a member of the Association of University Presses.

First printing 2022
∞

Library of Congress Cataloging-in-Publication Data available

LCCN 2021056988
ISBN 9781496836441 (hardback)
ISBN 9781496836458 (trade paperback)
ISBN 9781496836465 (epub single)
ISBN 9781496836472 (epub institutional)
ISBN 9781496836489 (pdf single)
ISBN 9781496836496 (pdf institutional)

British Library Cataloging-in-Publication Data available

Books by LeAnne Howe

Shell Shaker. San Francisco: Aunt Lute Books, 2001.

Equinoxes Rouges. Trans. by Daniele Laruelle. Paris: Lethielleux, 2004.

Evidence of Red: Poems and Prose. Cambridge, UK: Salt Publishing, 2005.

Miko Kings: An Indian Baseball Story. San Francisco: Aunt Lute Books, 2007.

With Janice Acoose, et al. *Reasoning Together: The Native Critics Collective*. Norman: University of Oklahoma Press, 2008.

Edited with Harvey Markowitz and Denise Cummings. *Seeing Red: Hollywood's Pixeled Skins—American Indians and Film*. East Lansing: Michigan State University Press, 2013.

Choctalking on Other Realities. San Francisco: Aunt Lute Books, 2013.

With Doireann Ní Ghriofa. *Singing Still: Libretto for the 1847 Choctaw Gift to the Irish for Famine Relief*. Privately printed chapbook, 2017.

Savage Conversations. Minneapolis: Coffee House Press, 2019.

Edited with Padraig Kirwan. *Famine Pots: The Choctaw-Irish Gift Exchange, 1847–Present*. East Lansing: Michigan State University Press, 2020.

Edited with Joy Harjo and Jennifer Foerster. *When the Light of the World Was Subdued, Our Songs Came Through: A Norton Anthology of Native Nations Poetry*. New York: Norton, 2020.

Contents

Introduction

I've always wanted to be thought of as a female Will Rogers pointing out ironies and absurdities for a bilious public. Hubris made me say this, forgive me!
—LeAnne Howe

In her 2017 interview with poet Jeremy Reed, Choctaw writer LeAnne Howe jokingly compares herself to the famed Cherokee performer, writer, and humorist Will Rogers. Despite her tongue-in-cheek apology, laying the blame on "hubris," the comparison is apt. Like Rogers, Howe was born and raised in Oklahoma as a citizen of one of the southeastern tribes forced westward as a result of the Indian Removal Act of 1830 (Biography). Many of the fourteen interviews in this collection, ranging from 2002 to 2020, are punctuated with laughter, as Howe jokes about subjects that aren't really funny but that she paints in a humorous light: commodification of American Indian cultures, stereotyping of Native peoples, and even misreadings of her own work. Jen Shook's 2020 interview, in which she focuses on Howe's life-time of performance and playwriting, emphasizes the vaudevillian elements in Howe's writing, another connection to the famed Cherokee performer and jokester.

Not included in this book is LeAnne Howe's most visible interview, her 2007 appearance on Jon Stewart's satirical news program, *The Daily Show*. In this interview, Aasif Mandvi asks her questions about Chief Illiniwek, the University of Illinois's official fake Indian mascot, which had just been retired after seventy years. Howe, who taught at Illinois for nine years, represented the American Indian Studies (AIS) program, a counterpoint to the non-Native "Fighting Illini Tribesman" who defended the former mascot while wearing orange and black face paint, presumably designed to make him appear warlike. In her 2012 interview with David Davis in the *Society for the Study of Southern Literature Newsletter*, Howe describes the fallout from the Board of Trustees' decision to retire the mascot on the faculty members in the AIS program: "The American Indian Studies building on the Illinois campus is periodically threatened. Someone calls and leaves a voicemail threatening to blow our building to smithereens. Swat teams came to our building in 2007, and in 2011, our director of American Indian Studies, Robert Warrior, and his family were threatened by a voicemail left on our office phone." Yet, on Stewart's show, Howe is hilarious as she speaks with Mandvi about the irony of campus outrage at the "removal" of Chief Illiniwek and even gives Mandvi an "Indian burn" as evidence of her expertise. I asked her about this moment in our 2013 interview, published as the appendix to my book, *LeAnne Howe at the Intersections of Southern and Native American Literature*. Howe responded, "Why do I know how to do that? [*Laughs*] Aasif said, 'Give me the Indian Burn.' [*Makes Indian Burn sound effect.*] He said, 'Oh, that really hurt!' I said, 'Why do both of us know what that is?' And we laughed. Yeah, wasn't that wild?"

As funny as Howe's appearance on *The Daily Show* is, it is not included in this volume because the interview is ultimately not about Howe or her work, but it is a fine example of her humor, her ability to laugh at herself, and her fearlessness when it comes to critiquing the social problems that have stemmed from the history of European and US settler colonialism in the United States. With the exception of Mandvi's, *Conversations with LeAnne Howe* includes every published interview to date with the Choctaw author.

The book begins with Golda Sargento's 2002 interview, originally available on the Aunt Lute Books website. Aunt Lute has published three of Howe's books: *Shell Shaker, Miko Kings: An Indian Baseball Story,* and *Choctalking on Other Realities*. The press is probably most famous for publishing Chicana feminist Gloria Anzaldúa's *Borderlands/La Frontera*, but her work is just one example of how the press has been "bringing revolutionary queer women, women of color, and underrepresented voices to the forefront of literature since 1982" (Homepage). Sargento's interview focuses primarily on the movement through time in *Shell Shaker*, which had just been published the previous year. In many ways, this first short interview presages what will come in *Conversations with LeAnne Howe*. Though *Shell Shaker* is her first novel, it is the subject of more questions than any other of her works in the interviews that follow, a testament to the award-winning novel's powerful themes and well-crafted plot. Sargento also asks about Howe's use of history in her novel, an element that will continue in all of her published books of poetry, fiction, and drama over the next two decades. Another aspect connecting this interview to other interviews in the book is Howe's discussion of the Middle East, where she had lived previously and where she would live again as a 2010–2011 Fulbright Scholar in Amman, Jordan. Her 2013 travelogue, *Choctalking on Other Realities*, speaks to her global travels, and this is a subject of particular interest in Howe's interviews with UK scholars Rebecca Macklin and Padraig Kirwan in 2016 and 2017. As Kirwan's interview in *Women: A Cultural Review* notes, "Howe appears to be especially interested in the representation of travel, exchange, contact, and consumption not only in the precontact and postcontact United States, but also within the global village."

It is notable that there is a gap between Sargento's 2002 interview and my first interview with Howe in 2008; the other twelve interviews follow in fairly quick succession, from 2010 to 2020, speaking to Howe's prolific output during these two decades and the increasing scholarly interest in her work. My 2008 interview in *MELUS* dug deeply into questions of gender roles and Choctaw religious and cultural practices in both *Shell Shaker* and *Miko Kings*. LaRose Davis's 2010 interview from *Wicazo Sa Review* delved even more into the historical elements of *Miko Kings* and the African American–Native American connections in the novel, especially its setting at present-day Hampton University where Davis and Howe met at the university's annual Read-In. That year, *Miko Kings* was chosen as the Read-In selection, the first time a book written by a Native American author held that honor. Davis notes that the selection of *Miko Kings* "presented an unprecedented opportunity for Hamptonians to grapple with the history of the school's Indian program and how that history shaped the contemporary institution." Both my *MELUS* interview and Davis's *Wicazo Sa Review* interview underscore the qualities of Howe's writing that reflect the values of Aunt Lute Books and demonstrate why the press includes her work alongside many great women of color writers including Gloria Anzaldúa, Alice Walker, Paula Gunn Allen, and Audre Lorde.

In literary critical circles, LeAnne Howe is well known for her theory of tribalography, first introduced in the 2002 essay "The Story of America: A Tribalography," an explanation of Indigenous storytelling that "comes from the Native propensity for bringing things together, for making consensus, and for symbiotically connecting one thing to another" (42). Howe continued to develop this methodology as "embodied tribalography" detailed in essays published between 2013 and 2015. Half of the interviews in this collection explore Howe's neologism to some degree; in his 2016 interview, Padraig Kirwan asks Howe if she had envisaged the impact that the term would have on the field, such as the journal *Studies in American Indian Literature* devoting an entire 2014 issue to the methodology. Howe expresses surprise but also pleasure at the impact her ideas have had: "So, that's been really delightful—that I've been helpful to people trying to understand the way that Native people tell stories, and *what we want.* We want, I think, reciprocity." In Jeremy Reed's interview, he asks Howe about the impact of using multiple genres, and Howe explains the connection of tribalography to her creative process: "My career has been a tribalography, my term for the way American Indians tell stories—in multiple genres." This theme is expanded upon in Jen Shook's discussion of the way Howe's 2019 book, *Savage Conversations*, has been talked about by reviewers. She highlights Nathan Scott McNamara's classification of Howe in the *Los Angeles Review of Books* as a "genre chemist," describing *Savage Conversations* as "a play/poem/novel/historical nightmare."

Howe's vision of "embodied tribalography," or the way that Indigenous peoples embody the places from which they originate, manifests in how she talks about her and her tribe's relationship to land in the US Southeast and in Oklahoma. Both my 2008 *MELUS* interview and my 2013 interview with Howe delve into her relationship to southeastern lands, especially the Choctaw's emergence place—their mother mound, Nanih Waiya, in Winston County, Mississippi. Both David Davis, in the *Society for the Study of Southern Literature Newsletter*, and Gina Caison, in her podcast *About South*, ask Howe to talk more about her position as a writer of the "Native South" and to delve into her own interpretation of the term, which has emerged over the last two decades to classify the field of southeastern American Indian and Indigenous studies. In her interview with Davis, Howe describes the Choctaw's continued relationship to the Nanih Waiya, emphasizing Indigenous kinship with the land: "We visit our birthplace in the South because the land is also our family." When asked to define the "Native South" in that same interview, Howe sidesteps the question, focusing instead on the field of Native studies. In my 2013 interview, Howe hones in on the concept of "southeastern-ness," as connected to the Indigenous peoples of the region. When Gina Caison asks Howe to define and discuss the usefulness of the concept of the "Native South," Howe explicitly rejects the term: "I think the Native South is an academic fiction in and of itself. I think that because maybe it lacks a southeastern component. It's the South, well, yeah, the South is many things, but the southeastern South, our original homelands, are places in which Native people believe we still have purview over the land, and our mother still calls us to return."

Oklahoma is another homeland Howe discusses in these pages. My third and final interview with Howe, "'An American in New York': LeAnne Howe," probes Howe's relationship with the land in the state where she grew up and her history there. She shares stories of her Cherokee and Choctaw families, including their connections to that land as Indian Territory and during the extreme challenges of the Dust Bowl. We also unpack the ways she brings Oklahoma into her work such as her personal connections to the character Lena in *Miko Kings*. In her interview, "Genre-Sliding on Stage with Playwright LeAnne Howe," Jen Shook, an Oklahoman herself, talks to Howe about their ambivalent relationship to that place. Howe calls it the "the Frankenstein of states" because it was "cobbled together in a really ugly way," referencing the history of how Indian Territory and Oklahoma Territory were merged. Shook and Howe also expound upon the current artistic interest in Oklahoma, discussing a number of recent depictions including the HBO series *Watchmen*, as well as new variations of the musical *Oklahoma!*, and their divergences from the original play by Cherokee writer Lynn Riggs. Howe is in the process of coauthoring a poetry collection with Dean Rader about their home state, and she notes that one of their aims is to try to understand "what makes Oklahoma Oklahoma."

Embodied tribalography also manifests in Howe's creative projects on mounds that evolved from the multiyear grant she received from Canada's Social Sciences and Humanities Research Council, along with Monique Mojica and a number of other scholars and artists. Howe talks extensively about mounds in these interviews and the ways they intersect with her work including in my 2013 interview, Kirwan's interview, and Shook's interview. She explains to Kirwan that the play she cowrote with Monique Mojica, *Sideshow Freaks and Circus Injuns*, "has its roots in [her] Aunt Euda's performing Indian in the circus. We found that synergy and noted that when the exhibitors put on the World's Fair in St. Louis in 1904, they destroyed sixteen mounds to put up a Ferris wheel!" In her 2019 conversation with CAConrad on the podcast *Occult Poetry Radio*, Howe describes many of the mound sites she visited in North America as part of her research and some of the spiritual encounters she had in those places. She explains to Conrad that these "are sites of powerful energy, and visiting these sites, really taught [her] about the different kinds of energy because like human beings or like anything else animate, not all mound sites are good. They're not, they can be powerful for various reasons—their purposes are known unto them because they are alive, just like we are."

Conrad's interview, my 2019 interview, and Shook's interview are useful for comprehensively exploring Howe's work as a poet and playwright. Given that the majority of the interviews in this collection (as well as scholarship on Howe's work) focuses on her novels *Shell Shaker* and *Miko Kings*, exploration of her poetics and her long history as a playwright is much needed in Howe criticism. Shook's interview provides the most sustained conversation about Howe's incubation as a playwright and performer with her early collaborator, Roxy Gordon, in Dallas-Fort Worth during the 1980s. Each of these three interviews also explores the creation and impact of Howe's 2019 book, *Savage Conversations*, and gleans insight into the 2020 collection, *When the Light of the World Was Subdued, Our Songs Came Through: A Norton Anthology of Native Nations Poetry*, that Howe coedited with Mvskoke/Creek citizens Joy Harjo—poet laureate of the United States—and Jennifer Foerster.

"'An American in New York': LeAnne Howe," the penultimate chapter, is connected thematically to many of the other interviews in the book, but it also stands apart as the only interview in which Howe is asked to elaborate on personal, biographical subjects. We explored the topic of her pseudonym "LeAnne Howe" (her legal name is Izola Wilson) and its impact on her life; her abandonment by her Choctaw birth mother and her adoption by a Cherokee family when she was five days old; and her concerns that she might have what was previously called Asperger's syndrome (now defined as being on the autism disorder spectrum), which manifested in the character of Ezol Day in her novel *Miko Kings*. Perhaps most painful of the revelations in this interview is that her adopted mother married a schizophrenic man who tried to kill her and her family. At this moment in the interview, I couldn't help but think of Joy Harjo, Howe's longtime friend and coeditor of the *Norton Anthology of Native Nations Poetry*. In Harjo's memoir, *Crazy Brave*, she describes her traumatic childhood with an abusive father and stepfather. Later in life, as a mother, she hides with her children when her estranged partner drunkenly attempts to break into her house and threatens to kill her. It is a brave act to share this kind of personal trauma, but it also helps us to understand how artists and writers are formed. Howe notes that there are themes of running away in her work that stem specifically from her feelings of childhood trauma and abandonment, hearkening back to Harjo's own connections of overcoming trauma when she wrote her first (and now renowned) poem, "I Give You Back," about releasing her fear.

The interviews in this collection illuminate LeAnne Howe's kaleidoscopic way of connecting seemingly disparate images and moments, what Dean Rader described as "connectedness among appearing disconnects" (ii). You can see it on display in the Chronology of this book, authored by LeAnne Howe, who jokingly called it her "Allocution." For example, Howe describes the following events as occurring in 1963: "Adopted father tries to kill Mother, brother, and me with a butcher knife. He drinks Drano and is hospitalized at Central State Griffin Memorial Hospital. Diagnosis: homicidal schizophrenic. President Kennedy is assassinated." Personal tragedy in an Oklahoma Native community is juxtaposed with a national tragedy that has often been parsed as the end of an era of hope. In my 2013 interview with her, I asked Howe about the juxtaposition of local Choctaw events to national tragedy and the way she had foregrounded tribal history in her work, especially in *Miko Kings*. Howe described how what might have been an epitomizing event for the dominant culture was not necessarily one for her or for her community. Yet this chronology also spotlights Howe's ability to laugh at life's absurdities, as she shared with interviewer Jeremy Reed when she compared herself to Will Rogers. For example, in the years 1959–1961, Howe notes that she "Attends third grade at Putnam City School in Warr Acres, Oklahoma. Marvin, the kid living across the street on Hatley Drive in Bethany, screams, 'Fuck you.' I tell on him. We get in trouble. Him for saying it, me for hearing it." Howe's irreverent story of a loss of childhood innocence might not seem immediately relevant in the story of her life, yet she asserts that it is through her telling. Her humorous approach echoes the "poignant philosophy and timeless humor" of vaudeville's "Man from Oklahoma" (Rogers and Wertheim 21). These interviews display the complexity of a writer who cannot be put into one category. LeAnne Howe is a poet, playwright, novelist, theorist, documentarian, performer, jokester, and sometimes all of these things at once. She is also one of the most influential American Indian voices of the twenty-first century, as evidenced by her prolific publications over the last two decades.

It has been a pleasure and an honor to edit this book, which would not have been possible without LeAnne Howe's gracious willingness to give her time and thoughts in both formal interviewing settings and informal conversations in person and via email. Not only did she participate in two new interviews specifically for this collection ("'An American in New York': LeAnne Howe" and "Genre-Sliding on Stage with Playwright LeAnne Howe"), but she also worked tirelessly to help me edit those interviews and give feedback on other parts of the book. Interviewing Howe has been one of the great joys of my scholarly life, evidenced by the fact that all three of my interviews with her are included here. My first interview with Howe, conducted in 2008 and published in *MELUS* (2010), was also my first national publication; not only did I learn much about Choctaw lifeways and her writerly worldview from that interview, but I also learned the ropes of academic publishing. In addition to my appreciation of all that LeAnne Howe has contributed to this book, I gratefully acknowledge the work of my two research assistants:

Meagan Pusser (High Point University) and Megan Brown (East Carolina University). Meagan Pusser worked with me during the summer of 2018 to transcribe and format interviews, and Megan Brown transcribed and formatted interviews during my tenure as Whichard Visiting Distinguished Professor in the Humanities at East Carolina University from 2019 to 2022. I deeply appreciate the Whichard Professorship at ECU and High Point University for funding my research. I also want to thank Indigenous literature scholar Steven Sexton for his thoughtful feedback on this introduction. Lastly, I am grateful for the support of my husband, Andy, and my son, Jake, as I worked through sunny summer days to complete this book.

KLS

Works Cited

Biography. *Will Rogers: The Official Website of Will Rogers*, CMG Worldwide, 2020, https://cmgww.com/historic/rogers. Accessed 26 June 2020.

Harjo, Joy. *Crazy Brave: A Memoir*. W. W. Norton, 2013.

Homepage. *Aunt Lute*, Aunt Lute Books, 2018, https://www.auntlute.com/. Accessed 26 June 2020.

Howe, LeAnne. "The Story of America: A Tribalography." *Clearing a Path: Theorizing the Past in Native American Studies*, edited by Nancy Shoemaker, Routledge, 2002, pp. 29–48.

McNamara, Nathan Scott. "Eyes Cracking like Egg Yolks: LeAnne Howe's 'Savage Conversations.'" *Los Angeles Review of Books*, 20 February 2019, https://lareviewof books.org/article/eyes-cracking-like-egg-yolks-leanne-howes-savage-conversations/. Accessed 26 June 2020.

Rader, Dean. Foreword. *Choctalking on Other Realities*, by LeAnne Howe, Aunt Lute Books, 2013, pp. i–vii.

Rogers, Will, and Arthur Frank Wertheim. *Will Rogers at the Ziegfield Follies*. U of Oklahoma P, 1992.

Squint, Kirstin L. *LeAnne Howe at the Intersections of Southern and Native American Literature*. Louisiana State UP, 2018.

"Trail of Cheers." *The Daily Show with Jon Stewart*, Comedy Partners, 2020, http:// www.cc.com/video-clips/mzzn9f/the-daily-show-with-jon-stewart-trail-of-cheers. Accessed 29 June 2020.

Chronology

LeAnne Howe

This chronology was created by LeAnne Howe for the book, as noted in the introduction.

1951   Born Billy girl, April 29, 1951, in Edmond, Oklahoma, to Christine Billy, Choctaw. Adopted on May 4, 1951, and driven to Ada, Oklahoma. The home is still in the family.

1955   Family adopts a white baby boy. He develops hepatitis from a poorly sterilized needle used for vaccinations at the doctor's office. He nearly dies.

1956   Contracts scarlet fever in 1956 and cannot attend kindergarten.

1957–58   Attends Skyline School, Bethany, Oklahoma. Reads *Fun with Dick and Jane* in first grade. Should have read it in kindergarten. Attends second grade in Bethany. Teacher Miss Griggs reads *Black Beauty* each day. Summer at Cherokee grandmother's house in Ada.

1959–61   Attends third grade at Putnam City School in Warr Acres, Oklahoma. Marvin, the kid living across the street on Hatley Drive in Bethany, screams, "Fuck you." I tell on him. We get in trouble. Him for saying it, me for hearing it. Contracts rheumatic fever and misses the fourth grade. Hospitalizations. Heart murmur. Moon face from fat deposits on the sides of my face and all over my body from massive doses of cortisone. Taken to Ada to heal at Cherokee grandmother's house.

1961–62   Family moves to Moore, Oklahoma. Repeats fourth grade in Moore, Oklahoma. Reads *Heidi*. Summer at Cherokee grandmother's house in Ada.

1963   Sixth grade in Moore, Oklahoma. Adopted father tries to kill Mother, brother, and me with a butcher knife. He drinks Drano and is hospitalized at Central State Griffin Memorial Hospital. Diagnosis: homicidal schizophrenic. President Kennedy is assassinated.

1964–66   Struggles in Moore. Adopted father regularly breaks out of Central State Griffin Memorial Hospital in Norman, Oklahoma, and hitchhikes to Moore with a kitchen knife. For two years, Mother, brother, and I sleep on a hideaway couch in the living room in case he breaks in.

1967   Moves with Mother and brother to Midwest City, Oklahoma, to a small house under the flight pattern of Tinker Field Air Force Base. Attends Midwest City schools.

1968   Adopted father dies. Mother remarries. She and my brother move to Wiesbaden, Germany, with our stepfather, an Air Force sergeant. I remain in Midwest City. Works at various jobs.

1969–70   Begins waitressing for SkyChefs, Inc. On the nightshift at Will Rogers World Airport earning $1.15 an hour. Join the union AFL-CIO. Receive a nickel an hour raise to $1.20. On October 7, 1969, at 2:15 p.m. a Super Sabre training jet crashes into Glenwood Housing District on Bowman Drive where I live. Houses on fire. Windows blow out. Pilot lands in my front yard, copilot dies. Unscathed, my dog and I escape. I decide to become a writer and go to college. My older son, Joseph, is born in 1970.

1972–75   Attends South Oklahoma City Junior College in Oklahoma City, now Oklahoma City Community College (OCCC). Transfers to University of Oklahoma for classes. My younger son, Randall, is born in 1972. Later transfers to Oklahoma State University, Stillwater. Moves to Texas.

1976–77   Production Manager, *Performance Magazine*, Fort Worth, Texas.

1978   "Children" published in *The Chariton Review*, Volume 4, #2, edited by Jim Barnes.

1978–80   Editor in Chief. Created and developed along with partner Sheree Turner *Worth Magazine*, Fort Worth, Texas.

1981–91   The dead years. Worked in plastics factory, sometimes wrote plays, short stories, and sometimes worked as a waitress.

1986   *Coyote Papers* published by Wowapi Press, Dallas. Chapbook. Short stories.

1987   *A Stand Up Reader* published by Into View Press, Dallas. Chapbook. Short stories. *Big PowWow*, three-act play coauthored by Howe and Roxy Gordon. Staged and produced by Sojourner Truth Theater, an African American theater company in Fort Worth, Texas. First collaboration between American Indians and African Americans in Texas. April–June 15, 1987.

1991   "Moccasins Don't Have High Heels" and "The Red Wars" both appear in *American Indian Literature,* Revised Edition, University of Oklahoma Press, edited by Alan Velie. "The Bone Picker" appears in *Fiction International* #20 edited by Clifford Trafzer. "Dance of the Dead" published in *Looking Glass,* University of California's Publications in American Indian Studies, edited by Clifford Trafzer.

1992   "Danse de l'amour, Danse de mort" published in *Earth Song, Sky Spirit: An Anthology of Native American Writers,* Doubleday & Co., edited by Clifford Trafzer. Winner of the Pen Oakland Josephine Miles Award.

1993   *Indian Radio Days* directed, rewritten by Howe for radio. Performed by WagonBurner Theatre Troop throughout the Midwest at colleges and universities and at CSPS Theater in Cedar Rapids, Iowa. Also broadcast on American Public Radio stations throughout the Midwest and uplinked via satellite to Alaska Public Radio stations on Columbus Day 1993.

1994   "The Chaos of Angels" published in *Callaloo,* Native American Literature, Volume 17, #1, Native Heritage Issue, Johns Hopkins University Press. "A Story for Ohoyo Shatanni" published in *Returning the Gift: An Anthology,* University of Arizona Press, edited by Joseph Bruchac.

1995   "Moccasins Don't Have High Heels" appears in *Native American Literature,* HarperCollins College Publishers, edited by Gerald Vizenor.

1996   "Shell Shakers" appears in *Story,* F&W Publications, Volume 44, #3, edited by Lois Rosenthal.

1997   "Indians Never Say Good-bye" appears in *Reinventing the Enemy's Language,* W. W. Norton, edited by Joy Harjo and Gloria Bird.

1999   *Indian Radio Days,* three-act play in *Seventh Generation: An Anthology of Native American Plays,* published by Theatre Communications Group, edited by Mimi D'Aponte. "Tribalography: The Power of Native Stories," essay in *Journal of Drama and Theatre,* University of Kansas.

2000   *Indian Radio Days* coauthored by Howe and Roxy Gordon. Directed by Cameron Ulrich, performed at the University of South Dakota, in Vermillion, with a thirteen-member cast. November 8, 2000. "Blood Sacrifice" and "A Story for Ohoyo Shatanni" appear in *Through the Eye of the Deer,* Aunt Lute Books, San Francisco, edited by Carolyn Dunn Anderson and Carol Comfort. "Blood Sacrifice" is chapter two of my novel *Shell Shaker*. MFA in Creative Writing awarded in January 2000, Vermont College of Norwich University, Montpelier, Vermont (now Vermont College of Fine Arts).

2001   *Shell Shaker* published by Aunt Lute Books, San Francisco.

2002   *Shell Shaker* honored with an American Book Award 2002 from the Before Columbus Foundation and Wordcraft Circle Writer of the Year, Fiction, 2002.

2003   *Shell Shaker* a finalist for Oklahoma Book Award 2003.

2004   *Équinoxes Rouges* (French translation of *Shell Shaker*) published by Roucher, Collection Nuage Rouge, Paris. Finalist for 2004 Prix Médicis Étranger Award.

2005   *Evidence of Red* published by Salt Publishing, Cambridge, UK. Poetry.

2006   *Evidence of Red* honored with Oklahoma Book Award for Poetry, Oklahoma Libraries Association, and the Oklahoma Center for the Book. Winner 2005–2006 Wordcraft Circle Writer of the Year. On-camera narrator and screenwriter, *Indian Country Diaries: Spiral of Fire*, ninety-minute PBS documentary airing nationally on all PBS affiliate stations throughout November 2006. A coproduction of Native American Public Telecommunications and Adanvdo Vision. Part memoir, part tribal history, the film takes me on a journey to reconcile my identity as the daughter of a Choctaw mother and a Cherokee birth father I never knew.

2007   *Miko Kings: An Indian Baseball Story* published by Aunt Lute Books, San Francisco.

2010   J. William Fulbright Scholarship awarded for residence in Amman, Jordan, 2010–2011.

2011   Tulsa Literary Trust Award, Tulsa Tri-County Library's American Indian Author Award.

2012   Lifetime Achievement Award from the Native Writers Circle of the Americas. Ceremony, Milwaukee, Wisconsin. Named USA Artist by USA Artists Foundation, Los Angeles.

2013   *Choctalking on Other Realities* published by Aunt Lute Books, San Francisco, September 2013. *Seeing Red: Hollywood's Pixeled Skins—American Indians and Film*, published by Michigan State University Press, edited by LeAnne Howe, Harvey Markowitz, and Denise Cummings.

2014   Inducted into the 2014 OCCC Alumni Hall of Fame. Modern Language Association (MLA) awards its first biennial prize for Studies in Native American Literatures, Cultures, and Languages to *Choctalking on Other Realities.*

2017   Five weeks' rehearsal and performance of a play, cowritten with Monique Mojica. *Sideshow Freaks and Circus Injuns* performed as a staged reading at CIT, Downtown Toronto, directed by Spy Welch. Canada Council Grant. *Singing Still: Libretto for the 1847 Choctaw Gift to the Irish for Famine Relief,* chapbook, coauthored with Irish poet Doireann Ní Ghriofa, winner of the Lannan Literary Prize, poetry 2018.

2019   "The Gift," poetry and song chants taken from *Singing Still: Libretto for the 1847 Choctaw Gift to the Irish for Famine Relief.* Performed by an ensemble of four performers, directed by Stephen Gardner. Opening night concert for *The Gift,* Wednesday, May 22, 2019, at Strokestown Park and National Famine Museum, Vesnoy County, Roscommon, Ireland. *Savage Conversations* published by Coffee House Press, Minneapolis. Book is the story of Mary Todd Lincoln and the "Savage Indian" she created to physically torture her in 1875.

2020   *When the Light of the World Was Subdued, Our Songs Came Through: A Norton Anthology of Native Nations Poetry,* featuring two centuries of Indigenous poetry, edited by Joy Harjo, LeAnne Howe, and Jennifer Foerster. *Famine Pots: The Choctaw-Irish Gift Exchange, 1847–Present,* coedited by Padraig Kirwan and LeAnne Howe. Four Choctaw scholars, four Irish scholars discuss the 1847 Choctaw gift of money for Irish Famine Relief. Foreword by the President of Ireland, Michael Daniel Higgins, and the Choctaw Nation of Oklahoma Chief, Gary Batton.

2021   *Searching for Sequoyah,* PBS Documentary film, fifty-six minutes, Coproducer and Writer LeAnne Howe, Coproducer and Director James M. Fortier, a PBS and Vision Maker Media film. Aired nationally on PBS and all affiliates, November 2021. Story of Sequoyah, his life, and how he created the Cherokee Syllabary, first written language in the New World.

Conversations with
LeAnne Howe

An Interview with LeAnne Howe

Golda Sargento / 2002

From the Aunt Lute Books website, www.auntlute.com, August 2, 2002. Reprinted by permission of Joan Pinkvoss, Executive Director, Aunt Lute Books.

Author of *Shell Shaker*, LeAnne Howe has worn many hats, shape-shifting from a Wall Street securities investor to a plastic champagne glass factory worker, from waitress to journalist, from radio host to novelist, scholar, and world traveler. But one of the first things you might read about her is that she's an enrolled member of the Choctaw Nation of Oklahoma. LeAnne has delivered lectures, performed plays, and read short stories from the Middle East to the Midwest, along with teaching in Native American studies classes, hosting her own radio program, and having her plays produced in New York and Los Angeles. Most recently she has taught at Carleton College, Grinnell College, Sinte Gleska University on Rosebud Sioux Reservation, and Wake Forest University. She wears red. LeAnne was recently awarded a Before Columbus Foundation American Book Award for her first novel, *Shell Shaker* (Aunt Lute, 2001), which follows the Choctaw Billy women through generations of events to unravel an unresolved moment in Choctaw history. She researched many years to tell this story, and though the story is fiction, her setting and even some characters are based on recorded history. The following is an interview with LeAnne, as she reveals bits of her process and her shift to the world of novelists.

Golda Sargento: What was it like writing a novel based on historical facts?

LeAnne Howe: In writing *Shell Shaker*, I wanted to remain faithful to some of the historical events in the eighteenth century that continue to influence the Choctaw present. Daniel Boorstin has labeled these kinds of events as "pseudo-events," meaning that there is agreement that something happened in history, but a disagreement as to its significance or how it plays out within a specific cultural group. The event I considered most important, historically, for the Choctaw was the assassination of war chief Red Shoes in June 1747. He is murdered after the sun goes down on the evening of the summer solstice, his head is taken, and soon afterwards a Choctaw civil war ensues.

GS: Why did you choose to set the novel in the present?

LH: Because contemporary Choctaw life remains tied to past events. How those events still resonate in modern Choctaw society interested me very much. So, in 1991, there is a character named Redford McAlester who is chief. He wants to control the way foreigners (corporate America and the federal government) interact with Choctaws in much the same way Red Shoes wanted to control the English and French in the eighteenth century. Redford McAlester starts out being a fairly good leader, but something happens. He becomes obsessed with power and his demise is certain. It's an old story. Look around you in California—at your modern political or corporate leaders. Take Richard Nixon, or historically closer to home, the masterminds of Enron. Now you know who helped create California's energy crisis last summer. Just because *Shell Shaker* is about the Choctaws, it should still resonate with people from mainstream societies.

GS: Having written both plays and essays and lectured throughout the country and abroad, you are a very visible member of your community. What have you found in your experience as a voice for your people?

LH: Well, I never think of myself as a voice of the Choctaw. I am a Choctaw woman, and I have political opinions that I voice. But one thing remains constant in my travels: that no matter whether it's South Dakota or Japan, people still know almost nothing about Indigenous issues in America, know nothing about tribal people or Choctaws.

GS: Have you had a different experience with your novel than with, say, your academic essays?

LH: That's hard to say. Academic arguments are meant to be, well, argumentative, so that debate can begin. This is a healthy thing about the academy. However, a novel or story is meant to be experienced in a different way, so people respond through the experience of my characters. Characters are experienced very differently from ideas.

GS: Turning towards current events, you have lived in the Middle East. Any thoughts about the current situation?

LH: Only incredible sadness. I think both sides, Jews and Palestinians, must be willing to give in to each other, to offer each other sanctuary. That is what a real homeland is, isn't it? A sanctuary where children can grow. But so far this is not even a consideration. I'm hardly an expert, just someone who spent a year there, so I feel that my small opinions don't stand for very much.

GS: What are some of the things Native American authors are dealing with in the world of fiction?

LH: That, even today, we have survived in spite of all the things that have been done to us. How that survival plays out is in the next chapter.

Golda Sargento is an artist residing in the Bay Area.

Choctawan Aesthetics, Spirituality, and Gender Relations: An Interview with LeAnne Howe

Kirstin L. Squint / 2008

From *MELUS* 35, no. 3 (Fall 2010): 211–24. Oxford University Press on behalf of Society for the Study of Multi-Ethnic Literature of the United States. Reprinted by permission of Kirstin L. Squint.

To begin sifting through the mélange of humor, resistance, and intellectualism that shoots through the work of Choctaw poet, novelist, playwright, screenwriter, essayist, and scholar LeAnne Howe, it is helpful to examine the author's photograph on the back cover of her collection *Evidence of Red* (2005), winner of the 2006 Oklahoma Book Award for poetry. Playfully smiling, Howe salutes the camera, emulating a similar move by the giant wooden Indian behind her. The wooden Indian is adorned in what appears to be a loincloth of stars and stripes and a sign that reads "Cigars Cubains." Howe's choice to pose in front of the cigar store Indian, a symbol of the original trading relationships between Natives and Europeans that ultimately led to colonization, genocide, and the commodification of the American Indian image, is a joke on anyone who thinks that Native peoples are conquered, "vanished," or frozen in time. Indeed, a number of Howe's Choctaw characters literally time travel in her books, creating opportunities to overcome oppressive histories with returns to homelands or reversals of defeats.

Shell Shaker, Howe's first novel, was published in 2001 to critical acclaim. It received an American Book Award from the Before Columbus Foundation (2002) and was a finalist for the Oklahoma Book Award (2003), and its French translation, *Equinoxes Rouges*, was a finalist for France's Prix Médicis Étranger (2004). The novel moves between the eighteenth century and the present, linking eras through the actions of Shakbatina, a ceremonial shell shaker whose self-sacrifice on behalf of her daughter becomes an act that resonates across centuries to unite the Choctaw tribe, split by the 1830 removal from the Mississippi homelands to what is now Oklahoma. Poet and literary critic Ken McCullough claims, "Although there has been significant scholarship on this historical period in the southeast, between the arrival of de Soto and Removal, no one has written a work of the imagination (of this magnitude) set in this period" (61). Howe's work is meticulously researched, revealing the complexity of ancient trade relationships between southeastern Native peoples, the complications that ensued when European colonial powers arrived in the Americas, and the manifestation of these historical moments in the lives of contemporary Choctaw characters.

Howe's second novel, *Miko Kings: An Indian Baseball Story* (2007), also shifts between past and present, unraveling a family mystery set against the backdrop of all-Indian baseball leagues and detailing the love affair between Choctaw pitcher Hope Little Leader and Justina Maurepas, his Black Indian lover. This relationship suggests an intersection between Native American and African American histories of oppression and displacement: the characters meet at Hampton Normal School for Blacks and Indians (present-day Hampton University), and their affair ends after terrorization by the Ku Klux Klan. As *Shell Shaker* works to heal the wounds of Choctaw colonization and dispersal, *Miko Kings* recenters the ball game known as "America's pastime," illuminating its roots in Choctawan spiritual and political traditions.

In addition to her fiction, poetry, and scholarly work, Howe wrote the screenplay for and narrated the ninety-minute PBS documentary *Indian Country Diaries: Spiral of Fire* (2006); and her play *The Mascot Opera: A Minuet* was commissioned for the 2008 production at the Mixed Blood Theatre in Minneapolis, although it was not used. Howe has been the recipient of numerous artistic awards and residencies, including the Louis D. Rubin Jr. Writer-in-Residence at Hollins University; an Artist-in-Residence grant for theatre from the Iowa Arts Council; a Regents' Distinguished Lecturer at the University of California, Riverside; and in 2006–2007, she was the John and Renee Grisham Writer-in-Residence at the University of Mississippi at Oxford. Howe is currently a professor of American Indian Studies and English at the University of Illinois at Urbana-Champaign. Her creative work has been informed by her academic pursuits, but there are also strands from her years as a journalist, government bond trader, and actress. Both of her novels brim with a variety of characters, including stock brokers, college professors, warriors, spirits, baseball players, political activists, physicists, and gamblers.

In April 2008, I interviewed Howe at the Society for the Study of Southern Literature Biennial Conference in Williamsburg, Virginia, where she was an invited reader. Howe read from *Miko Kings*, which had just been published the previous year and, like *Shell Shaker*, is partially set in the lower Mississippi Valley, the ancient homelands of the Choctaw peoples. The interview focused on these two novels, particularly their representations of Choctawan cultural elements such as spirituality, linguistic characteristics, ancient trade and diplomacy practices, and gender roles. We also touched on debates in contemporary American Indian literary criticism; this area of discussion was partly inspired by the previous night's lecture by Craig S. Womack,[1] Howe's participation with Womack and others in *Reasoning Together: The Native Critics Collective* (2008), and my own interest in potential links between Native American critical theory and postcolonial theory. What follows is a result of that initial 2008 conversation and email discussions throughout the early part of 2009.

Kirstin L. Squint: Let's begin with *Shell Shaker*. The book has an enormously diverse cast of characters, from eighteenth-century Natives to differing southeastern tribes to contemporary figures who range from stockbrokers to actresses to college professors. How did you perceive your audience as you were writing the novel?

LeAnne Howe: There are no non-Natives, almost none, in *Shell Shaker*, and that's on purpose, because this is a discussion that I wanted the Choctaw characters to have with one another. There was a large section of the novel that I removed because it was not about the Choctaws. I had written a lot about the French in 1690–1724, and those chapters were deleted, because I ultimately wanted this to be our story. A Choctaw story. Yet, at the same time there is Jean-Baptiste Le Moyne de Bienville, founder of the French colony in New Orleans and colonial governor of Louisiana. In the story, the FBI makes an appearance, as do the Irish and Italians. I am trying to show that there are people who are collaborators in the process of colonization and the people who work against it—which is typical of reservation or Indian community life, Indigenous community life, Native community life—however you want to say it. So that is the work that *Shell Shaker* does—at least I hope so.

I'm conscious of the fact that there are spirits in the text, animal spirits and ancestors' spirits. There are also walk-ons, characters that are non-Natives. Certainly, the Italians are underdeveloped characters. But the story is not about them. It's about the situation that we Choctaws have been put in. And there's a good reason there are Italians. First of all, the Genovese family tried to infiltrate Indian gaming. I took that piece of the novel right from newspaper accounts back in the early 1990s. But the Italians are not integral to this work. Mainly, it's a book that interrogates Choctaws past and present.

KLS: In *Shell Shaker*, Adair discusses how the Choctaw people have been internally colonized, and there's a really great discussion of that related to the Queen Anne dining table. Do you see your books as artistic productions that use decolonization tactics?

LH: Well, I think I try to do some of that work. The dining table scene is one example. This is also the same process at work in *Evidence of Red* and in *Miko Kings*. For instance, there is another example in *Shell Shaker* when Bienville walks into the Choctaw camp and talks with Shakbatina's daughters Haya and Anoleta. Haya is a child, and Bienville begins speaking with her, and I believe that Haya says something like "He's speaking very well." She's trying to compliment him to her sister who despises him. Shakbatina has already told us that Bienville speaks Choctaw like a baby. That's another place in the text where I'm trying to show that the French or the English or Spanish didn't speak our languages "perfectly" as the historians have said they must have. The foreigners spoke like babies, and in the case of the French, the Choctaws treated them like babies and tried to give them things. That is also tied into another conversation in *Shell Shaker* where Delores Love is trying to talk about the Choctaw mother mound, the Nanih Waiya, and the ancients who are stuffed into burial mounds in that same area. You see all these trade goods that are buried with them because they've been dug up by archaeologists and anthropologists. In these scenes, I am trying to ask if the scholars might have misunderstood the meaning of burial goods. Oftentimes archaeologists have said, "Oh, this person must be an honored leader" because look at all the things that were buried with him. Or her. Well, actually, from a Native community standpoint, hoarding "things" means that you're selfish. So I wrote what that hoarding might have been about with the character of Red Shoes and Redford McAlester. He has a sickness called greed. That's another intervention in the text. I'm suggesting that the archaeologists might have misread the meaning of elaborate grave goods. Our word *Naholla* means "stingy."

These are interventions in the story where I'm trying to say, "Think about your perceptions of Native people. Perhaps the images you have of us, the stereotypes, and even the histories you've read might be incorrect." I'm saying, "You've misread the mounds, you've misread what those burial ceremonies might be, you've misread how we treated you because you act like babies—I want, I want, I want." In every chapter, I've tried to say, "You've misread us." Delores Love, one of the aunties, illustrates this. As does Isaac Billy. In one scene, Isaac tells the story of those birds and the incident at Fort Rosalie and how, in the retelling by historians, the story has been misread. The Natchez come to Fort Rosalie to give these amazing trumpeter swans to the French officers in charge of the fort. A Frenchman shoots this mated pair, this gift, and calls them worthless waterfowl. That comes right out of the French colonial documents about why that incident occurred. This is another instance where I'm saying, "You've misread what these 'worthless waterfowl' meant to the Natchez people, and you've killed them." Isaac retells that narrative to explain where Fort Rosalie was located, next to the mating grounds of these trumpeter swans. Shooting the pair of swans enraged the Natchez and they attacked the fort. This is the truth of this story, and the Natchez, of course, must move into the Chickasaw towns. Why? Because we must preserve life, not destroy it. Red Shoes acted as the *fani miko* to the Natchez to try and save them from the French, and many did move into Chickasaw towns.

KLS: What does *fani miko* mean?

LH: It's a speaker for the opposing tribe. Like a diplomat, but not exactly. The role is perhaps more dynamic.

KLS: There have been some debates by Native scholars about the applicability of postcolonial theory to American Indian literature, particularly hybridity theory. Good examples of these debates are Jace Weaver's, Craig Womack's, and Robert Warrior's discussions in *American Indian Literary Nationalism*. I'm curious about your thoughts on this issue, specifically Homi Bhaba's conception of a third space that tries to offer an alternative to the binary of colonizer and colonized.

LH: I don't think it is applicable, per se. Choctaws are most famous for being much more dynamic in their diplomacy, more than third spaces, more like sevens. [*Howe draws an image of three points that are connected on a sheet of paper.*] Imagine this is a foot stool. You see this. [*Howe indicates her drawing.*] It's never a binary in our relationships with other peoples and tribes. When you look at trading negotiations between communities— whites don't exist as part of the equation in these discussions at this point— I'm talking about the 1540s. These kinds of relationships are what you find in the Southeast when you delve into the Spanish records. [*Howe again points to her drawing.*] You see, it's a triangle. And those triangles morph into clusters, mound cities, and transnational cultures in the Lower Mississippi Valley. I refer to them as Seven Sister communities in the novel, and if one keeps traveling east up past the Alibamu towns, there would have been hundreds of different communities that lived in a region, but they are often ceremonially different from one another. Some of the languages tend not to be Muskogean. There are different language groups, all pivoting around these triangles, circles within squares like on Mississippian conch shells, and geometric configurations. They traded, intermarried, and played ball-games with each other. What I'm suggesting in *Shell Shaker* is that these very ancient communities had vibrant intertribal relationships. That's what I think is most important. There are no binaries—good guys, bad guys—in the Lower Mississippi Valley.

What is Indigenous theory and how did it work in our communities? I think Native scholars and even non-Native scholars working in American Indian Studies are making good headway about defining what it was in the past and what it is today. I also think it's helpful for the United States federal government to look at our Indigenous epistemologies as a way to forge more organic governances in the twenty-first century. Southeastern Natives, Indigenous people, have always been interested in uniting, not dividing. In that way, we can be helpful in getting our country past the nightmare of binaries that the Bush administration has created. I'm talking about the rhetoric of "do-gooders versus evil-doers." What I am trying to say in my novels and poems is that, in the Southeast, Choctaws or Choctawan peoples were successful for ten thousand years in making relationships. It wasn't a paradise; it was fraught with many tensions. But we're still here despite all attempts to wipe us out.

KLS: Your concept of tribalography seems to suggest an aesthetic of unification, the idea that people from diverse lands and periods of time can come together through storytelling, such as the story of the Haudenosaunee's confederation that inspired the US founding fathers. Both of your novels are layered with movements toward unification. Do you see your novels as forms of tribalography, and how does this differ from or intersect with a Western approach to the novel form?

LH: Yes, I do try to write what I call tribalography. I take the position that Native literature, American Indian literature, First Nations literature is foundational. Our stories are holding up the sky that mainstream novelists are flying in. I think American novelists are moving toward our understanding of literature. It's the way we tell stories that American writers have adapted to, not the other way around. Look at all the contemporary novels that do exactly what Native stories have always done. They take a community of people. The discussion of [Toni Morrison's novel] *Paradise* could be one example that Craig Womack gave last night. He was talking about Toni

Morrison's work but also teeing off of the way Natives tell stories. Typically, there's not a single protagonist, but rather a community of characters or choir of characters that is necessary to tell a story. I gave this same lecture at the University of Illinois a few years ago. If you begin to position Native literature as foundational, what you begin to see is American novelists, wholly American novelists, Black and white, Asian, moving toward Native ways of storytelling. Take a look for instance at the American novels in the last twenty-five years that began to use a splintered storytelling style with multiple characters and multiple points of view. They're not linear. This is the land teaching people here how to understand and talk through that space. So, in my way of thinking, contemporary writers are just now catching up. American literature is moving toward a more tribal, tribalography space, and that's the way that we can then see the growth of the American aesthetic. It's based on Indigenous ways of telling, not the other way around, in which American Indians have become assimilated enough to have learned to tell stories just like white people. That's the perception out there in Book Land.

KLS: I'd like to talk about the ceremonial aspect of *Shell Shaker*. Did you intend for Shakbatina's ceremony to be a healing ritual, and how did you see it working to heal on both individual and cultural levels?

LH: Which ceremony?

KLS: The one in which she travels through time to help Auda.

LH: Don't you mean her bone-picking ceremony, which comes later? There are multiple stages of ceremony storied through Shakbatina's character. First of all, there is her death in the first chapter. That, too, is a ritual ceremony when her head is bashed in by a man from the Red Fox town. The event sends a message of her sacrifice to both communities. Through her death, Shakbatina makes the path white, makes peace, between the two tribes, the Choctaws and the Chickasaws. You should investigate Lex Talionis; it's the French pronunciation. The Choctaws and other southeastern tribes had what was known as a kind of blood revenge. A lot has been written about that, but that is what happens in the first chapter of the book. Nevertheless, that exact scene, her execution by the Red Fox elder, is in itself a ceremony and a ritualized ceremony for that other woman's death. Each step of the way for Shakbatina is a ceremony. So her sacrifice you see in Chapter One continues in later chapters. In the next scene she is watching over her community, and then you see her again in this moment of bone-picking with her husband, a warrior from a different moiety—that's an old-fashioned term. That is also a ceremony of continuing to heal. The bone-picking ceremony releases her to move into yet another ceremony where she exacts revenge against the chief who walks out in front of the eighteen-wheeler—Tonica. When you see this beginning and ending, that too is the ceremony working its way through the book.

KLS: Could you talk a bit more about traditional shell-shaking ceremonies?

LH: Not all Choctaw towns had shell shakers. Certainly now, Choctaws by and large don't shake shells. Some communities did in the ancient or distant past. [*Howe draws a map that covers most of the southeastern US.*] When you look at our confederacy a long time ago, you see this, this handle here, along the coast, and we'll pretend this is the Mississippi, and this would be part of Louisiana up into what would become the Tensaw or Tennessee here. You see this confederacy all the way over into here. These are fabrics that changed over time, so when you think about the Choctawan confederacy, we stretch from here to here, and certainly here in Mobile [*Howe points to the map.*] Mabila, a language and a town, would be here. You could think of them as daughter villages, one after the other. Look at the maps in Patricia Kay Galloway's text *Choctaw Genesis*. I think she's done a wonderful job, especially introducing maps from the de Soto era through the French period. We deeply disagree over some things, but I think her work with maps and her translations are excellent. And I have learned a great deal from her research. Some of these older communities within the confederacy at one time shook shells; some did not. Because of our family alliances with Chickasaws and Creeks, some communities and people do shake shells, but by and large, Choctaws do not. That is something we lost before Removal, but I'm seeing Choctaws taking it up at others' grounds in Oklahoma. I'm also suggesting certainly that the seven sisters that are in the first chapter were Choctawan, and they were shaking shells. That's the point of those scenes in the novel. There are essences of older people and older ways, previous to our Removal from the Southeast, written into the novel. The scenes were really about trying to recover some of the larger confederacy that existed. That's really what I was trying to do in the hope that this book, this text, read by my own community, will help other Choctaws remember their own stories, so that they might bring more of the past back into existence. And that's the way tribalography, the method, works. One thing leads to another, and through the chain of stories we are able to grow stronger.

KLS: Both of your novels deal with intersections between historical and contemporary figures. In *Shell Shaker*, this is possible through a series of century-crossing ceremonies, and in *Miko Kings* it's possible through a physics that is connected to Choctawan linguistic elements. I'm not sure if you would put it that way.

LH: That's right.

KLS: These events suggest a permeability of history and time. How do these intersections of past and present represent a Choctawan worldview?

LH: Mainly because Choctaw language is almost always present tense and moving. That's one thing. It's another reason why I consciously write in present tense even though I'm writing about the past. For almost all of us Native-centric types—my tongue is in my cheek—the past is ever-present whether it's through the ceremonies, ghosts, or land. Think of it, land is past tense and present tense at the same time. The land actually is a wonderful space in physics that is all things at once—past, present, and future—so for me, I can't imagine a worldview without it or without action that unites all these things at once. And I think because the American narrative is very young, the national narratives are very young, too. Americans have trouble articulating Natives in the national narrative other than to say that we have vanished. Convenient, since the national narrative begins around 1776. But for Indigenous people that's not even yesterday. But as I say, I think mainstream Americans are growing toward our aesthetic whether they realize it or not. They always have. Look at American Indian art. American Indian art created the aesthetic of modern art. It doesn't exist without the foundation of Indigenous people's art. Especially beginning at the turn of the last century. To define American modern art, folks had to build off of Indigenous designs. It's the same with story. Literary studies are now at least looking at Native aesthetics. That's a start.

KLS: Regarding language, Ezol says in *Miko Kings* that Choctaws and Europeans have different views of time because Choctaw language represents time differently, and Lena says that Ezol based her hypothesis on language theory. This reminds me of Saussurian linguistics in which he posits that language creates a world external to itself through its very description. Is Ezol's theory coming primarily from traditional Choctawan cosmology, or do you see her as a syncretic character who blends the scientific theories of her era with Choctawan epistemologies?

LH: Ezol is talking about verbs. That is what she is saying. This is certainly part of the Choctawan epistemologies. I'm saying flat-out that speech acts create the world around us. And those are primary, foundational. We can look at verbs and verb tenses, especially in Choctaw, as a way of moving the mountain through the act of speaking. That speech act is as powerful as number theory to nuclear physics. Many non-Indians put all their faith in numbers, the power to add them up to create or destroy. Natives, I think, on the other hand, put our faith in speech. What is said. That's why if you speak of death to an individual or a thing, you make it happen. So we don't speak of some things because it's that powerful, especially the voices of women. In that way, my narrative in *Shell Shaker*, as I see it, goes back to Choctaw women. I'm trying to say that the power of speech is evoked through the way we use language and verbs. That is what Ezol is trying to say in *Miko Kings*.

KLS: Women are key figures in both of your novels. Isaac Billy in *Shell Shaker* discusses the traditional matrilineal system of Choctaw culture. In *Miko Kings*, the Four Mothers Society is an important political organization. How has the patriarchal structure of the colonizing European culture impacted the matriarchal culture of the Choctaws historically and in the present?

LH: I probably don't think it has a deep core value. I do know that one of my colleagues, Associate Professor Michelene Pesantubbee, a religious studies scholar at the University of Iowa, disagrees with me. From my read of the documents, Choctaws always put males out in front to "sacrifice themselves" if need be when meeting with people from a different group or tribe. So that does not suggest to me that Choctaw women have lost their negotiating status. Whites, or more correctly, eighteenth-century Frenchmen, were just one more different group that Choctaws intended to trade with. Then as the eighteenth century progressed, we became surrounded by difference. But today, there isn't an organization—this is where Michelene and I don't agree—or community group at home that isn't run or managed by women. You want something done, go to the women. I see that as a continuance of something very old. Who is at the head of my family? I am. I'm the oldest girl. This remains true today as it was in the past. Certainly, it was true with my aunts until they all passed. Now, I don't mean to suggest a kind of essentialism, but maybe that's what I am guilty of doing. I admit I'm talking about my own family and my own novel here, but women run things in our communities. I think we still are people who have maintained our culture as we change to meet the new centuries sprawling before us.

KLS: Your emphasis on matriarchs in your novels—could this also be read as a decolonization tactic in the sense that it reminds, maybe not Choctaw readers, but definitely Euro-American readers of the power of matriarchal culture?

LH: Well, I'm speaking to both, I guess. I don't necessarily think that I'm *just* speaking to Choctaws. I don't think I'm *just* speaking to whites, Blacks, or Asians either.

KLS: I couched the question that way because I was originally assuming to some extent that patriarchy had overwhelmed matriarchy, and so I was wondering if this is a way to remind Choctaws of matriarchal culture as well, or do you see it more as a representational aesthetics?

LH: Actually, I do see it as representational. I mean, how would you say that we don't?

KLS: I read an article by Kay Givens McGowan that suggested that, for those southeastern tribes that were matriarchal, patriarchy has subsumed them.

LH: I think this is something that Michelene assumes too, and that Choctaws had a beloved woman society and now it has collapsed. I don't agree. But I don't want to take anything away from her scholarship, and we're certainly friends; we just don't see this issue the same way. I don't think that Choctaw women are subsumed by patriarchy.

KLS: That's not your experience.

LH: No. Today we say, "Okay, if your relatives were on the Dawes rolls," we will recognize you as an enrolled member of the Choctaw Nation. In the past we reckoned kinship by the mother's family. Now, over time if you had a male or female relative on the Dawes rolls, the tribe recognizes you as a member. But it's funny. I was recently with a group of Chickasaw women who were going to China. Who represented the people? Women. What group is out there on their way to wherever? Women. Who are the matriarchs of the families? Women. Who are at the grounds for ceremony? Women. Who creates the people? Women. Who is at the center of the family? Women. How would you explain Wilma Mankiller's twelve years as Chief of the Cherokee Nation? Joyce Dugan's four years as Chief of the Eastern Band of the Cherokee Indians? How do we explain that? What I'm saying is that the power of the woman is not dead in the Southeast. Follow our politics.

KLS: In *Miko Kings*, the relationship between Justina Maurepas and Hope Little Leader exemplifies the common history of oppression shared by African American and Native Americans, especially their meeting at the Hampton Normal School for Blacks and Indians. Why did you want to develop this theme in this novel, a novel that on the surface focuses on the roots of baseball and the culture of America's first peoples?

LH: Baseball is a diplomacy game and is, especially at its roots, exemplary of intertribal diplomacy. It's a game that promotes alliances and love affairs: men and women meet there at the ball fields from different tribes. It made sense to me that Blacks and Indians at Hampton Normal School would fall in love at school or on the ball field. The Owl family, Cherokees, married with African Americans at Hampton. I wanted to have a character resonate with New Orleans again in *Miko Kings*. Justina, or Black Juice, was that character for me in *Miko Kings*. This is really about saying in the novel that New Orleans was once part of the Indigenous homelands of Choctawan peoples. Certainly, Choctawans were living for eons all around New Orleans, and Justina/Black Juice's cousin, Bo Hash, is Houma. So, for me, our relationships with Black people in the eighteenth century were commonplace, as they are today. That's really what I was trying to say in the love affair between Hope Little Leader and Justina/Black Juice. Love affairs between Blacks and Indians are no different than those between whites and Indians. And they are just as longstanding, existing since we began taking in enslaved runaways from the French. About 1720, maybe before. Don't hold me to that date. It was not as big a deal as people make it out to be. I also wanted to talk about the Klansmen coming into Indian Territory and wanting to penalize some Choctaws for intermarrying with Blacks, and then scaring the shit out of Blacks or killing them for intermarrying with Indians. I wanted to show that Blacks and Indians are in that same space. In the novel, when the KKK people attack Hope and Justina's house, Choctaw ball players go out and try to chase them down with just a baseball bat and a shotgun. It's another reason why Ezol begins reading *Evangeline* to Justina, because she's trying to say that we will always be passing each other in these spaces.

KLS: Characters from Louisiana and events taking place in Louisiana figure prominently in both of your novels. Is this a way to remind readers of the traditional homelands and trading routes of the Choctaw, or do you have other reasons for using that setting?

LH: Louisiana is part of our ancient homelands. Hundreds of place names in the state are Choctaw. Atchafalaya is one good example. And what did we do when we came to Oklahoma or to Indian Territory? Just about every place name in Louisiana and Mississippi was transferred and then renamed in our new homelands, now the state of Oklahoma. Even the names of people. Tannehill, where my family is from around McAlester, Oklahoma, is one example, and there is also a Tannehill, Louisiana. Tupelo, Mississippi, becomes Tupelo in Indian Territory, now Tupelo, Oklahoma. Every place name is renamed by the people. Nanih Waiya in Mississippi is Nanih Waiya, the lake at Tuskahoma, Oklahoma. Why is that important? The Choctaws took handfuls of earth from the land around the Nanih Waiya, our mother mound in Mississippi, as they began their journey on the Trail of Tears. When we brought our earth, when we brought our people, the names came with us. The Choctawan names are thousands of years old. The names. So the *falaya*, the long of it, is renamed. And that's to remind us and remind the people who live in our territories today, who are newcomers, that we are from ancient places; we are people who sprang up out of the Lower Mississippi Valley.

KLS: In *Miko Kings*, there's a character known as an Ohoyo Holba, "like a woman but not," who has healing powers. Can you discuss the traditional role of homosexuals and/or transvestites in Choctaw culture and contrast that to the role of gays and lesbians in contemporary US society?

LH: I don't think gays and lesbians are the analogue for Ohoyo Holba. I'm trying to say that Ohoyo Holba was not necessarily homosexual, but many things, including homosexual. Often they weren't just involved with other men but had many levels of relationships. They were also involved with our community in very special ways. They could be healers. They're people that protected our children because they embodied more than one thing. And what is part of Choctawan aesthetics is that we revere things that are unusual. Different. When you look at the spirit that's connected in Ohoyo Holba, and when they put on that dress in olden times, they are saying "the embodiment of many." That is very different from any discussion of homosexuality mainstream Americans have. In my novel, Ohoyo Holba is discussed differently between the two characters, Kerwin and Hope. Kerwin is a ballplayer; he is a healer; he is attempting to try to find his own way in a contemporary society that doesn't recognize the spaces he lives in. I really don't think they are analogous to each other. I think that mainstream culture has a very different idea about "two spirit" and what it embodies. Read the work of Diné anthropologist Wesley Thomas. His work deals with Navajo or Diné culture, but it will not resolve the question about Ohoyo Holba because "one-size" does not fit all. Diné and Choctaw are also different cultures. Also, with the rise of fundamentalism, homophobia in Choctaw Country is on the rise. This pains me. The more Christian Choctaws have become, the more homophobic they've become. I really think this is the next area in which I want to "argue with my own community." Let us think clearly about our traditions. This is probably the next topic I'll be working on within my own community. I didn't grow up with homophobic people, at least I didn't think so. I grew up with people who could be Ohoyo Holba or women who were "half-boys." It is also my observation that people chose not to speak about certain things, spirits, traditions, etc. Not everyone is supposed to know everything, after all. Now we're back to the power of speech, breath, and mind. People were more careful with their words. This is a space I'm going to be moving into next in my new novel. I want to challenge my own community. A good thing, I think.

Note

1. Craig S. Womack is the author of the seminal *Red on Red: Native American Literary Separatism* (1999), which argues for a tribally specific approach to American Indian literary theory, as well as numerous other critical writings including *American Indian Literary Nationalism* (2006), *Reasoning Together: The Native Critics Collective* (2008), and the poignant coming-of-age novel, *Drowning in Fire* (2001). [Note and Works Cited are from the original publication.—Ed.]

Works Cited

Galloway, Patricia Kay. *Choctaw Genesis: 1500–1700.* U of Nebraska P, 1995.

McCullough, Ken. "If You See the Buddha at the Stomp Dance, Kill Him!: The Bicameral World of LeAnne Howe's *Shell Shaker.*" *Studies in American Indian Literature*, vol. 15, no. 2, 2003, pp. 58–69.

McGowan, Kay Givens. "Weeping for the Lost Matriarchy." *Daughters of Mother Earth: The Wisdom of Native American Women*, edited by Barbara Alice Mann, Praeger, 2006, pp. 53–68.

Weaver, Jace, Craig S. Womack, and Robert Warrior. *American Indian Literary Nationalism.* U of New Mexico P, 2006.

Womack, Craig S. *Red on Red: Native American Literary Separatism.* U of Minnesota P, 1999.

Womack, Craig S., et al., eds. *Reasoning Together: The Native Critics Collective.* U of Oklahoma P, 2008.

Unspoken Intimacies, *Miko Kings*, Hampton University, and Red-Black Convergences: A Conversation with LeAnne Howe

LaRose Davis / 2010

From *Wicazo Sa Review* 26, no. 2 (Fall 2011): 83–91. Reprinted by permission of the University of Minnesota Press.

In the last weeks of March 2010, the students, faculty, and staff of Hampton University came together for the annual Read-In, a twenty-two-year fixture of intellectual and cultural life at the school. The selection for this year's Read-In was LeAnne Howe's *Miko Kings: An Indian Baseball Story*; the novel was chosen in part because of the connections that the story has to the school.[1] The Read-In activities included a miniconference, in which both students and faculty participated, a book signing, and a keynote address delivered by Howe.

Miko Kings, as Howe describes it, is multiple novels, multiple stories, in one book. Framed around the narrative of Lena Coulter, a twenty-first-century travel writer, the novel follows her character as she researches and writes a story about Indian Country at the turn of the twentieth century. The catalysts for her project are the documents that she discovers in the wall of her Indian Country home. As Lena, the would-be author and central narrator of the novel, researches the documents, the stories of Hope Little Leader and Justina Maurepas emerge. Hope is one of the greatest pitchers that the Choctaws have ever known, and Justina is a legendary figure from the Black nationalist movement and a woman of mixed-race heritage: African, Indigenous, and European. The tie that binds these two characters, we soon discover, is their great intimacy, which has its roots on the grounds of Hampton Institute.

The choice of *Miko Kings* for the Read-In selection was significant. It was the first novel by a Native American author to be selected for the event. As such, this year's Read-In presented an unprecedented opportunity for Hamptonians to grapple with the history of the school's Indian program and how that history shaped the contemporary institution.

During the two-day event, I had an opportunity to sit down with LeAnne Howe to talk about the novel, Hampton Institute, and red-Black convergences.

On Hope and Justina, Love and Language

LaRose Davis: We are here today because your novel *Miko Kings* was chosen as the 2010 Hampton University Read-In selection. I want to start with the book and with you talking a little about what you think your novel is about. You mentioned in our other conversation that you believed that there were multiple novels and multiple stories in a single frame; for you, what is the takeaway? What do you want people to get from reading this book?

LeAnne Howe: *Miko Kings* is, first off, about a love affair. It's about a relationship that happened because of this colonialist manifesto of the Hampton experiment. It began, for me, here at Hampton. I mean, the germ of the story happened at Hampton. But the boarding school experience, that manifesto of "We are going to colonize you. We are going to take away your land. We are going to take away your bodies. We are going to take away your mind. We are going to take away your language. We are going to replace that, all of the things that you are, with ourselves"—that story is embedded in *Miko Kings*.

I started with the love affair to ground me here at Hampton, because Hampton begins, or it is a good model for the beginning of, the replacings. I'm replacing your language with English. I'm replacing your religion, or not even religion, your beliefs—it's not beliefs, it's a system of knowledge—with our knowledge. And you can go to the gravesite and look at all of the children of that experiment, here at Hampton, who lie dead, in the cemetery as monuments to that replacement narrative. They've lost their family connections.

All of those things are just like a ball when it's thrown. The fingers of God, or the baseball player in this context, have put the spin on the story. That's what I was working toward in *Miko Kings*, and that's why it's situated here, because the Hampton experiment was here, and that replacement narrative is still spinning out among our Native peoples in the twenty-first century.

Davis: You mentioned Hope and Justina's relationship and its connection to that replacement narrative that you are talking about. Are there other roles that you see that relationship playing? In my reading of the novel, what I find interesting is how this relationship that is not supposed to happen, that is not supposed to be, becomes a defining relationship for them—not only in terms of their love for one another but also in terms of how they choose to move forward and engage in their separate but similar activisms. How do you think about that particular relationship?

Howe: Well, if you notice, he idolizes her. In the beginning of their relationship, when you are introduced to this great love, she is older than he is, and he idolizes her as both teacher and lover. Because women, you know, they're at the center of a creative universe. He immediately idolizes the fact that she is his teacher or the teacher's aide. He recognizes the power of women through Justina. So those things are very fluid for him.

There's also a second reason that is unspoken. He never looks at, or sees, Justina as a Black woman or a red woman. He sees her as a woman, and he is compelled by the power of that connection—that spark between people, between human beings, between a man and a woman—and that's what he sees. He sees her. She's very intellectual, and he's playing with her. There's that spark of humanity between them.

Davis: So what you are saying is that, for them, for their relationship, there wasn't really a consideration of race, in the ways that race might have been considered at Hampton and in Virginia in the moment that their relationship developed. They moved beyond that to the core, to that spark of humanity, which can happen between any two people.

Howe: She is very aware of their racial divide. But she's flirtatious. She is interested in him, but she is aware of what those differences are. He, on the other hand, believes that if he becomes that ball player and earns a good living, he will be accepted by her. So part of his motivation for running away is that he has to prove himself.

Davis: We can talk, I think, for a long time about her being more cognizant or aware of the taboo in some ways, which sort of sheds a different kind of light on her ultimate choice to leave both Hope and Indian Country. Perhaps she leaves because of the awareness that she always had that there was something forbidden, disallowed, about the relationship—the societal perception that there is something about this relationship that should not be.

Howe: But she did not know that either as a child. She's just older than Hope. Remember, her father is a Frenchman, and she wasn't aware of race either. She knew that he looked different. There were people in and out of the house. Her family is very politically aware, and they were a different class. All of that is destroyed, and she talks about that. She didn't know. She believes herself to be French. As a little kid, that's just the way things are. It's only after she is sent to Hampton that this is wrong, this is taboo, that she goes through that transition, because as a little girl she did not see race either. That's what I am trying to say with their relationship, that Justina is not unlike Hope, but she is a few years older than him and she gets it then. At the time that she is acting as a teacher's aide, she knows. She also has her own ideas about how the universe should be. That's the reason that she eventually goes into the Courtesan in Storyville in New Orleans and blows it up with a stick of dynamite, because she sees what's happening to those children of prostitutes. She's an activist, taking matters into her own hands.

So, in a way, [Hope] thinks that if he is a part of this team and he makes this difference, he is also going to be accepted by her. She thinks, on the other hand, that once she is in the environment of New Orleans, she has to make a difference. There are all kinds of things that play out in that age difference. There are all kinds of things that play out in their character motivations. In some ways, they are very much alike.

Davis: You talk also about language, and maybe we can go there next. Because I have some specific questions about the ways that I saw language working throughout the novel, and not just in terms of Hope and Justina, in the power of language to rewrite history. We see, rather frequently, meditations on the power of language in writing and specifically in Native American literature because of the relationship to the oral tradition and speaking as power. I wanted to talk a little about that because I saw it playing out in some interesting ways in terms of Hope and Justina's relationship and their retelling of their relationship. Were you thinking about that as you were writing?

Howe: About the power of language?

Davis: Well, about the power of language in the retelling and the recreation of that particular relationship. In terms of Hope and Justina telling the story of their relationship, and not only telling the story of their relationship, but Hope telling the story of that baseball game, right? At the end, he's telling that story and telling it differently; [I wonder] whether that has the power to change the original outcome.

Howe: Lena Coulter changes the outcome.

Davis: By recovering the story?

Howe: Right. Lena is the catalyst when she is called home. The land calls her home. It's time to come home. The land situates the story, and in some ways, Lena is recovering the story of the Miko Kings baseball team, and she also helps turn back time. That becomes both a metaphor and a truth of the game for Natives. As the ball spins out, there is the turning back of time when baseball is played.

What do we know about Choctaw language and verbs? That they have the power of changing the world. And I really think that we are only understanding what speech does to even the cellular structure of our own bodies. When we speak of health, we are able to change those things. When the chants happen, when the old man splits the clouds, when Ezol says documents lie, she is really talking change and change happens. It is both a metaphor and an event that happens in the novel. And it can only happen after Lena comes home and begins to unravel the story. She's spinning it out as well. Hope is able, then, to come back, play that game in that space and time, and make a different choice from the one that he originally made.

Let's take this to what we do as storytellers and writers, as academics, scholars, and investigators: when we do this same thing that Lena does, when we go back in our research, and through our work we undo or retell a wrong in the history books. In that way, we've turned back time. We've changed the world, or our understanding of the world, through our work.

Davis: So you are already changing it just in the retelling of it?

Howe: Right, and so we undo these events through our actions as storytellers. I am recovering Choctaw history that didn't exist until I wrote these things and told this story. It didn't exist. In effect, I have changed time and space. And that's the act of a writer, the act of a storyteller, the act of a scholar.

On Hampton as a Place

Davis: You said that part of your interest in Hampton was the replacement model that was a completion of the colonial project—e.g., we take the land and their places, and we replace them with ourselves and our places. Maybe you can talk a little more about what brought you to Hampton as a place.

Howe: Because of the Hampton method. For me, it isn't about the head, the heart, and the hand, and the hand comes first. It's about replacing everything that is inside of you with something else. . . . If we spin this out to literature, it's a zombie model. Everything you are, you must give up. Everything. And the pod people will be coming. There is a pod being made for you, and it looks like you, but is it you?

Now, why is Hampton so problematic for Natives? [Armstrong] brings the Apaches, you know.[2] The Apaches don't live here. This is not Apache land. This is not Dakota land. This is not Pima land or Tohono O'odham land. This is not Pawnee land. Ask yourself, why did they feel they had to go so far, if there were Natives living throughout Virginia? Could the answer be that you break the umbilical cord with their place, which you have to replace with something else? And it didn't work. There are no Dakotas that live here. Is this Dakota land? No. Is it Pima land or Tohono O'odham land? No. Is it Kiowa land? No. And we, the Choctaws, are not here. Who remains here in Virginia are the Virginia tribes; those tribal people are still here. And Hope, what is he doing once he's brought to Virginia? He's running away. He has to go back home. So Hampton, in the most base sense of the word, is dragging tribes *that will never be here* to this place.

I think there must be something that even goes beyond that. You know the Chiricahuas that the government brings up here to Virginia, the Apaches—they're not staying either. In their minds, this land belongs to the tribes that were here in Virginia. They instinctively understand that. You have to bring the whole tribe, as in removal. It's very, very difficult to work a colonial manifest one starving student at a time.

You know, people were being trained, excuse me, not just for labor, but to be domestic servants. What's up with the aprons and the hats? What is that, hmmm? That's servitude. If we look at the history of General Armstrong's family going out to take and conquer Hawaii, they are pretty base about who they think these colored people are. They're second class. They're not first class. They're not near first-class citizens. They're subjects, and that's what we remained. That's how I feel about Hampton. That they were subjects [to be] changed. I think that even the good intentions of the devil are still devilish intentions.

Davis: So when you are talking about bringing people here to begin that process of severing those ties to the land, to those places and people, of course then I have to think about African Americans and the African American experience, with the Middle Passage and that sort of thing. But then you say that neither of them could stay here. So, would you, then, say that New Orleans is Justina's place?

Howe: Well, it had been, but she's also mixed. Her family is mixed from Haiti. Yet her place that she knew, and that her tribe people in North America knew, is in Louisiana. And she, then, has relations that she knows and communicates with. What does she say at the end of her life? That her mother's life and her great-grandmother's life were far more interesting. Because she has made that journey, she has placed herself again in her own history. She's doing that work, also, of uncovering the self and where her lands and peoples are. So at the end of her life, she has done the same kind of work.

Davis: In thinking about Hope and Justina, how they came together and the reasons why they came together, do you think that one reason is because of the similar types of work that communities of color have to do? There are really two questions here. My reading of Hope and Justina's relationship places it as central to the novel and crucial to later decisions that they make. Do you see their relationship as having that same sort of centrality and power? Then, would you say that it is because we have to do similar kinds of work, as communities of color, to resituate ourselves in the places that we have been removed from, that the relationship has that type of impact?

Howe: Well, there are two things, I think, that I wanted to say and I believe my characters wanted to say. That this isn't about race; this is about people. Natives were having love affairs, making children, with whoever came along that they fell in love with, and there were no class or race distinctions in that way. We know that there are documents of having children with Spaniards who stayed, or British who came, or Africans who were escaping in the 1700s. [In] 1702, as soon as the French came, African people were running off from them and running into our communities. "OK, yeah, you can stay, if you want to be with us." So there's that. That we were always making children with whoever came along that we fell in love with, or whatever those relationships were. So that was one aspect of their love affair. And I also wanted to have characters that didn't just come together. They loved each other.

The second piece of this is that I saw them both having that work to do. They were kids. They had lost their families. In both cases, they had lost their mothers. In Hope's case, also his father. So, in some ways, they had to return [to those places] in order to complete their stories. And they both do that, in different times and in different ways. They have a juncture that is broken, that they are trying to repair.

It is clear, from my point of view and, more importantly, from my characters' points of view, that those junctures can be crossed between past, present, and future. The spirit is talking and speaking and narrating and affecting the future. The spirit affects the future, and so there are no endings in that way.

When the time is changed, their relationship is solid again and would have changed because he would never have thrown the game. Even in their various states of being, they are in connection. He sees her sitting in a chair. She feels him walk on the front porch. Their spirits are always in contact, and isn't that what love is all about? She feels his presence on the front porch of her house: a ghost is walking in. He's checking on her. He sees her in a chair. She's yawning. Those are spirit movements of the heart.

On the Read-In

Davis: Let's talk about being here and what you see as the usefulness of this event of Hampton collectively contemplating these histories that you are trying to recover with the novel. How do you feel about being back here for this event?

Howe: It's quite an emotional event for me. l was speaking to the chair of the department, and I was quite moved because I was here three years ago, [when] I was giving a talk at William & Mary. Allison Hedge Coke and I came together, and one of the graduates [from William & Mary] brought us to the graveyard. I had read about these students. We came and visited the graves, and we spoke their names out loud—again, this is back to speaking. We called them. We talked to them. We spoke their names. Every name of a Native student that we could find in the cemetery, we called it out. And I believe that part of this experience of being here is that by acknowledging them—from Native people acknowledging them—they called me back. It's because of them that I am here. That's it.

Davis: What have you thought, so far, about the ways that the Hampton community is responding to this novel and thinking about these histories?

Howe: I am quite moved. The students did a really wonderful job—the faculty did, too—about acknowledging what that time was about. I want to honor the people who made that possible. I hope that they continue, as an institution, to talk and realize that part of this history is about the sacrifices that those students, Black and red, made so that this institution might live.

Davis: What do you think is the potential, moving forward from this moment, in terms of reconciling and remembering that history in more complex ways that continue to have meaning?

Howe: Well, this is just an example. They have a Founder's Day celebration for General Armstrong, and they place a wreath near his grave every year. And I asked, "What about the wreaths for the children?" All of those are children, and there is nothing. Nothing. Now, once you look into the history of Hampton, the $127 [per child], I think approximately $127, represented the budget on which Hampton could operate. If you multiply it by the number of children brought here each year, some years it wasn't so good. He was also able to ask for donations for these children, so the Native American children were the industry that helped Armstrong build this institution. We talk about how the South was built on the backs of slaves. It was. This institution was also built on the backs of Native American children because the federal government would pay for them, as would many of the donors. So that complicates that history, and yet the only memorial is to the white man who came here. That seems to be . . . unsatisfactory.

Davis: It's true there isn't that acknowledgment of the Native American students who were here, but there also isn't really an acknowledgment of the African American students and the troubling ways that their bodies were used too for the creation and production of this institution. So even to move forward by just acknowledging that would be progress.

Howe: Some ways to acknowledge that history could be extended classes, curriculum enhancement—or how about having the students research just how many graves there are, what children were here, what happened to them, and what does "To lead and to serve" really mean in this nineteenth-century context? It means different things to different people. And it's not for me to say—you know, I am not at this institution—but it seems to be a question worth answering.

Notes

1. Hampton University is a historically Black educational and research institution in Hampton, Virginia, previously known as Hampton Normal and Agricultural Institute and later Hampton Institute. From 1878 to 1923, Hampton conducted a program that educated male and female Native American students alongside its Black students. The Native students were primarily from the Plains tribes, not from Virginia. See, for example, https://www.hamptonu.edu/about/history.cfm. Both notes with this interview were added by the editor. All bracketed insertions within the interview are from the original publication.

2. Samuel Chapman Armstrong was a former Union general and early leader of Hampton.

Interview with LeAnne Howe and Robbie Ethridge

David Davis / 2012

From *Society for the Study of Southern Literature Newsletter* 46, no. 2 (November 2012). Reprinted by permission of David Davis, Mercer University.

LeAnne Howe, a member of the Choctaw nation, is Professor of American Indian Studies, English, and Theatre at the University of Illinois. She is a prolific author, playwright, and scholar, and her many prize-winning works include *Shell Shaker, Evidence of Red, Miko Kings: An Indian Baseball Story,* and forthcoming in 2013, *Seeing Red: Hollywood's Pixeled Skins—American Indians and Film* coedited with Harvey Markowitz and Denise K. Cummings (Michigan State University Press) and *Choctalking on Other Realities: New and Selected Stories* (Aunt Lute Books).

Robbie Ethridge is Professor of Anthropology at the University of Mississippi. She is coeditor of the journal *Native South*; editor of *The Transformation of the Southeastern Indians, 1540–1760, Light on the Path: Anthropology and History of the Southeastern Indians,* and *Mapping the Mississippian Shatter Zone: The Colonial Indian Slave Trade and Regional Instability in the American South*; and author of *Creek Country: The Creek Indians and Their World* and *From Chicaza to Chickasaw: The European Invasion and the Transformation of the Mississippian World, 1540–1715.*

SSSL: What is "Native Southern Studies"?

LeAnne Howe: Native Studies has been an interdisciplinary program for the research and study of American Indian tribes. However, most American Indian Studies programs and departments are moving to change their names to Indigenous Studies. This is true in Canada and other programs internationally. One of the reasons is that by looking at colonial methodologies that were/are used on Indigenous peoples—well, everywhere—we're opening up the discipline to more potential confluences of research that will benefit students and faculty alike.

Robbie Ethridge: As an answer to this, I will take a page from the journal *Native South* and the position statement of the founding editors: me, James Carson, and Greg O'Brien. To paraphrase, Native Southern Studies is the investigation of southern Indians and their influence on the wider South and wider world. This, however, does not mean that such investigations are confined to the geographic area that was once the Confederacy, but includes "the area occupied by the pre- and postcontact descendants of the original inhabitants of the South, wherever they may be"—from the *Native South* masthead, 2012.

SSSL: How do the identity categories "Native" and "southern" overlap?

Howe: Three of the so-called Five Civilized Tribes constitute some of the largest American Indian tribes in the United States, and they're all from southern states. Consider the Choctaw Nation of Oklahoma with nearly two hundred thousand members. The Choctaw tribal towns originally stretched across Mississippi, parts of Alabama, Louisiana, and Florida; the Muscogee Creek Nation with sixty-nine thousand citizens is originally from Georgia, Alabama, Florida, and South Carolina; and the Cherokee Nation, the second largest tribe in the United States with over three hundred thousand enrolled citizens, originally from North Carolina, east Tennessee, and parts of Georgia. These tribes can all consider themselves "southern" because their original lands are in the South. I like to quote Paul Chaat Smith on this one. He's talking about the ways mainstream people see the National Museum of the American Indian in Washington, DC, and he contrasts it with how Indians see the museum: "One striking difference in how Indian audiences and many critics responded can be seen in the museum's insistence on mixing old objects with new, demonstrating its belief that the past lives in the present and conveying its overall message that we are still here," from *Everything You Know about Indians Is Wrong*, p. 99. In other words, for Natives, the past is always present. Our homelands are present tense for us, not someplace we immigrated from and forgot. So much of the writing by Natives and Indigenous peoples always references land. In this way, our identity is both.

Can a person be simultaneously Native and southern? Yes. I would expand my answer to include a question: can a person simultaneously be Jewish and American? If we agree that Jews in the United States can be both Jewish and American, and in some cases American Jews hold dual citizenship, that of Israel and the United States, then it seems possible for American Indians from the South to be Native and southern. By and large, Choctaws consider themselves southerners. Again, the reason is LAND. Our Choctaw Mother Mound is in Mississippi. The beginning of our existence as a people begins at our Mother Mound, the Nanih Waiya. It is our birthplace as a people, and as a Nation. Choctaws from Oklahoma regularly return to the Nanih Waiya in Winston County, Mississippi. We visit our birthplace in the South because the land is also our family.

I often ask students in my classes about their creation stories, and whether Jews, Christians, or Muslims they tend to say it's the Garden of Eden—there are, however, variations on the name. Then I ask where the Garden of Eden is located. They name a variety of places: Iraq, Turkey, Israel, or Iran. We talk about why all the confusion of locations. After a while I tell them that the birthplace of Choctaw people is in Mississippi at the Nanih Waiya, an earthwork with a cave nearby. "This is our creation story," I say, "and I can get in the car and drive to our tribe's birthplace. It is on the maps of Mississippi." We then unpack all the various ways of understanding what is important to people of various cultures. Native culture is less concerned with *when* an event happened than with *where* it happened. The place/land where an event occurred such as our tribe's birthplace is more important than at what century or date in the ancient past. I tell this story to illustrate that yes, we consider ourselves Choctaws, southerners, and southeastern tribal people. We are many things at once.

A note about Nanih Waiya. A few years ago, the Mississippi Band of Choctaw Indians in Choctaw, Mississippi, took over the site from the state of Mississippi to protect it and refurbish it. Though I walk on shaky academic ground here, I say, "with all the bias I can muster," to use Craig Womack's phrase from *Red on Red*, that the South and southerners would not, could not exist without American Indians, yet we are continually denied/erased, footnoted in the histories of the South. Why? Answer: LAND.

The descendants of tribes removed from the South are by and large still southern. Again, I would argue that southerners mapped on to Native and tribal lifeways—not the other way around. I also disagree with the linguists who say the southern dialect of English comes from Europeans. It's a ridiculous notion, really. When immigrants move to a new land, their children take on the speech patterns of the locals. Listen to southeastern tribal speech, the ways in which southern Indians speak. In our languages, the vowels are long and are song-speech, and consider the refrains: the repetition of certain rhythmic phrasings spoken by southern Indians. The story of how white southerners mapped themselves onto Native cultures *and* languages is another prong of research ongoing in Indigenous studies. Okay? By the way, Oke, Okeh, okay is a Muscogean word regularly used by southerners of all colors.

Ethridge: Yes, these identities can overlap, and they are not mutually exclusive. Identity, as we know, can be quite slippery, especially when one takes a long view of history. As indicated above, the idea of the American South is, itself, a product of history and largely defined geographically by the slave-owning states of the nineteenth century. Now if we accept that as a geographic definition of the South, with all sorts of caveats about porous borders and so on, we can then work to identify the original inhabitants of this geographic range. Then, it is a short step to identifying the descendants of these inhabitants. Interestingly, the Mississippian world (900 AD–1700 AD) overlays the antebellum South geographically because the requisites for corn and later cotton agriculture (and its auxiliary productions) were similar.

Having said that, though, identifying the original inhabitants of the South is not as easy as it may seem. For one, Indians have been living here for at least twelve thousand years, and precontact Indians were not static people: some left this geographic area at various times over those millennia, and others moved into this geographic area at various times over that long expanse of time. In addition, with the tumultuous years of colonialism, Native people made many long and short migrations across the continent. For example, increasing evidence indicates that the Quapaws are recent immigrants to the South, having moved from the upper Ohio River to the Arkansas River in the mid-seventeenth century where they displaced, most likely, groups of Tunica or Natchez speakers. Conversely, the Creek Confederacy only formed in the seventeenth century, yet they formed from an in situ foundation when precontact Mississippian polities fell in the wake of colonialism and survivors regrouped into the Creeks. They then took in people from distant locals like the Shawnees. Yet, I would still consider all of these people, including the more recent immigrants, to be southern Indians.

And then, of course, Indian Removal complicates this question even more. But as we said in our position statement for *Native South*, the descendants of the original inhabitants "wherever they may be." Are these descendants "southern"? I'd probably say no, but that doesn't mean they aren't of the Native South; it only means they don't currently reside here.

Reading LeAnne's response, I would only add that I had not thought of this in terms of origins. But I completely agree, that when one considers origins there is no doubt that one can be both Native and southern.

SSSL: How does Native history complicate racial construction?

Howe: The South is bigger than just the story of Blacks and whites, but the South has willful amnesia when it comes to American Indians. Indian boarding school experiments of mixing Blacks and Indians *together* begins in the South at Hampton Normal School for Blacks and Indians in 1878; earlier still, the study of early eighteenth-century Indian wars 1722–1746 reveals enslaved runaways came into our tribal towns and the formation of new kinship narratives both good and bad. The story is enormously complex. The Removal era beginning in 1830 reveals a much nastier racialized South in which peoples that are "red" are "removed"—that is, ethnically cleansed— so that southern whites could take over our former lands. Once we begin to study the race and culture of Natives in the South, we see, for example, the roots of the blues in Native call and response songs and in our stomp dances and even the roots of jazz. One of the projects that Joy Harjo, Muscogee poet and performer, is working on is how jazz came about through the music of Muscogean peoples.

Ethridge: That's a huge question. One thing is for sure, once you put Indians into the picture of the South, it explodes the binary Black-white construction, which I think is for the good. This has been a continued frustration of mine about southern studies—the study of the South is almost entirely predicated on a Black-white South, and it is a bulwark against any other sort of view of the racial complexity of the South. I always ask my non-Native students to take a minute and imagine "facing east," as Daniel Ricther has put it, and try to see the American experience through Native eyes. It looks really different, and the Black-white racial construction is usually the first thing to fall.

The interactions between Indians and Africans also have a long, complex history that defies the usual model of race and racism used in southern studies. Some really interesting recent works have been exploring how concepts of race and racism and Indian national sovereignty were intimately linked in the nineteenth century and how Indian people negotiated these tricky waters.

SSSL: Are the relationships among regional identity, tribalism, and transnationalism important to understanding the history, literature, and survival of Indigenous peoples in the South?

Howe: Yes. But I would state the question this way: are the relationships among regional identity, tribalism, and transnationalism important to understanding the history, literature, and survival of southerners, as well as Indigenous peoples in the South?

Ethridge: Yes. For one, these relationships belie the stereotype of the static, stuck-in-time Indian. Once we start to consider these relationships, we are forced to put Native people into history and to see that they, like everyone else, are products of history. The world became truly global in 1492, and

American Indians, like everyone else from that time forward, were and are part of this global system. Indigenous people around the globe change over time and continue to change with the historical and "prehistorical" winds. It's the case today, and it was the case in the past. Also, it's important to see that Indians, like most people, exist at the intersection of such relationships and one cannot take for granted or assume they know what it means to be Indian until one has examined these relationships. Indian people today and in the past forged their identities and affiliations out of this intersection. And I'll second what LeAnne said—these intersections form us all.

SSSL: How does Native Southern Studies cross disciplines? How are anthropologists, historians, literary critics, and other scholars working together? Could they work together more effectively?

Howe: Native Southern Studies needs a multidisciplinary approach to grow the field. Indigenous Studies utilizes multidisciplinarity when tackling research projects. An example of multidisciplinarity is a new book by Chadwick Allen titled *Trans-Indigenous: Methodologies for Global Literary Studies*. Allen analyzes Indigenous technologies like the Earthworks in Ohio, as well as Polynesian ocean-voyaging *waka*, cultures that are worlds apart, to offer new methods for the interpretation of contemporary Indigenous texts. In my own work, I cross disciplines working with archaeologists, cosmologists, physics, anthropologists, historians, and literary critics. It only makes sense in the twenty-first century.

Ethridge: How do we work together? I think we do an okay job, but we need to be able to talk across disciplinary lines better, which is sometimes difficult given the specialized jargon we all use—except, perhaps, for the artists. I think we also need to quit patrolling the disciplinary boundaries so much and give each other some leeway for making mistakes, etc., since obviously once one crosses the disciplinary boundary, one is bound to make some mistakes. My approach to interdisciplinary work is to begin with the question and then use whatever means we have at our disposal to answer it. If literary criticism helps answer a historical question, then use it. If archaeology helps answer a literary criticism question, then use it.

Scholarship on the Native South has been under way for several decades now, but I think only in recent years have we seen a convergence of the disciplines in addressing questions about the Native South. Certainly, the launch of the Native American and Indigenous Studies Association, NAISA, pulled together these various strands, and it now has a vital organization and conference where people can talk across disciplinary lines. Obviously, NAISA encompasses much more than the American South, but it does provide a forum for scholars of the Native South from various disciplines to converge, listen to each other, learn about each other's disciplines and work, and collaborate. NAISA is great for that.

In fact, we started our journal, *Native South*, in 2007 as a forum for interdisciplinary and multi-disciplinary conversations because we thought the time was right for such a thing. We publish across disciplines—history, anthropology, archaeology, literary criticism, sociology, education, public history, popular culture, linguistics, and so on.

We still have a way to go in doing truly interdisciplinary work, but I think we are on the right track, and we are already starting to see the fruits of these efforts in our classrooms and in our writing. For instance, I use LeAnne Howe and Linda Hogan in anthropology classes on Native North America.

SSSL: What are some of the challenges facing writers and scholars of Native Southern Studies? Are sufficient archival resources and publication venues available?

Howe: The biggest challenge facing writers and scholars of Native Southern Studies is willful amnesia. Racism on all fronts. We're footnotes in most texts on the South and Global South.

We face prejudices from our institutions as well. Just one small example by way of answering your question. I teach at the University of Illinois, and after the banning of Chief Illiniwek, the unofficial mascot is *still* Chief Illiniwek. The student organizations are still reprinting T-shirts with the chief's symbol and wearing them to our classes in a kind of defiance. The American Indian Studies building on the Illinois campus is periodically threatened. Someone calls and leaves a voicemail threatening to blow our building to smithereens. Swat teams came to our building in 2007, and in 2011, our director of American Indian Studies, Robert Warrior, and his family were threatened by a voicemail left on our office phone. Since I've joined the Illinois faculty in 2005, there have been three different administrations—presidents, chancellors, and provosts—all wringing their hands about how to keep us safe. I applaud their efforts, but very little is done. Perhaps no one can stop the harassment by Chief Illiniwek supporters on our campus. But this is just one example of institutional racism.

As to publication venues: there are many good venues for publication, and more journals are being developed all the time. NAISA is launching a new journal this year. *American Indian Quarterly*, *SAIL*, and *American Quarterly* are a few academic journals. Still, we are invisible in most mainstream journals. The Chickasaw Nation press launched a new press about five years ago, and it's publishing new texts each year. This is an exciting development.

The field is not difficult to periodize for Indigenous scholars. Consider the work of Matthew Gilbert, Hopi; Tol Foster, Muscogee Creek; Jodi Byrd, Chickasaw; Joanne Barker, Lenape; Robert Warrior, Osage; Jace Weaver, Cherokee; Craig Womack, Muscogee Creek; and Jane Hafen, Pueblo.

More tribal archives are being developed all the time. Currently, the Chickasaw Nation is developing its archives at the Chickasaw Nation's Cultural Center in Sulphur. That's one example.

Ethridge: It's funny—some of the biggest book awards in the country have gone to Native scholars and artists. But you can go to a history, anthropology, or southern studies conference, and there will be only a smattering of panels on Native studies, if any at all. You can pick up a conventional American history book and see the same old introductory chapter that basically says "Indians were here and then they were gone" before the author launches into an American story devoid of Indians. Southern studies still insists on a Black-white South, as does southern history and southern literature. Yet those of us who work in the field know that the story of America is a story of interactions between red, white, and Black.

I've thought about this so much my head is going to explode. I keep thinking, what is the hook, what can we do to get Indians into the mainstream of the American historical and cultural consciousness. I thought that the stellar works from Tiya Miles, Claudio Saunt, Theda Perdue, Celia Naylor, Fay Yarborough, and many others on the question of African slavery among Indians would have been the hook since southern studies and history seem obsessed with the question of Black slavery. But even these works go underutilized by the mainstream scholars.

And in anthropology, studying American Indians is almost passé or old-fashioned unless one is an Indigenous scholar. The reasons behind this are really complicated, but derive in part from anthropology's obsession with the "exotic" and "far away," and American Indians just aren't "exotic" enough or "far away" enough, or some such nonsense.

There are only a few venues for publishing journal articles—*Ethnohistory, Native South, American Indian Quarterly,* and a few others. I understand NAISA will be launching a journal, so that will help. However, publishing books seems a bit easier because the academic presses recognize that this is important work.

The periodization is a problem because the Indian experience has been so ignored in conventional studies and doesn't necessarily conform to the usual periodization. For example, Removal is an important moment for southern Indians, but that does not conform to the usual historical periods. Still, I think most of us find ways to work around this problem.

As for archival work, particularly in history and anthropology, there are few historical documents written by Native people, so we have to rely on documents written by non-Natives. This poses some peculiar challenges, but I think we have devised fairly decent ways of vetting these documents. We corroborate and amplify the documentary evidence with multiple lines of evidence from linguistics, archaeology, contemporary ethnographies, oral traditions, and so on. But still, in reconstructing the past especially, we will always have an incomplete picture because the evidence is uneven. But, as I always say, so what? I'd rather use this uneven evidence than let the story continue to go untold to the larger public.

Wow, LeAnne's story about her institution is chilling. This kind of racism is scary, and it can certainly get in the way of so many things, including having our work accepted by the larger academic and lay audience. It's all so disturbing, but I'm continually impressed by the courage of Native scholars, activists, artists, and others as they combat this sort of thing.

SSSL: Could you name some of the key texts for Native Southern Studies?

Howe: In terms of archives, I would suggest the Mississippi Provincial Archives: French Dominion, Vols. 1–5. The MPA: FD archives are full of great details about southeastern tribes. I suspect the readers of SSSL will know most of these references I give, so I won't go into detail. I recommend *That the People Might Live: Native American Literatures and Native American Community* by Jace Weaver; *Indian Literary Nationalism* by Jace Weaver, Craig Womack, and Robert Warrior; *Reasoning Together: The Native Critics Collective* edited by Craig S. Womack, Daniel Heath Justice, and Christopher Teuton; *Our Fire Survives the Storm: A Cherokee Literary History* by Daniel Heath Justice; *The Sharpest Sight* by Louis Owens; *Crazy Brave* by Joy Harjo; my own novel *Shell Shaker*; and an essay I published in 2001, "The Story of America: A Tribalography," in *Clearing a Path: Theorizing the Past in Native American Studies*. Of course, I loved *Red on Red: Native American Literary Separatism* and *Drowning in Fire* by Craig Womack. Both are fine southern literary texts. I love Robbie Ethridge's *Mapping the Mississippian Shatter Zone*, and I use *Hero Hawk and Open Hand: American Indian Art of the Ancient Midwest and South*, edited by Richard F. Townsend, as a text in my literature courses.

Ethridge: *Knights of Spain, Warriors of the Sun* by Charles Hudson. This book is the most complete and thorough reconstruction of the southern Indians at the time of European contact, ca. 1540, available.

The Indian Slave Trade by Alan Gallay. Here, Gallay opens up the story of the commercial trade in enslaved Indians that went on in the South for over a hundred years. I'll take this opportunity to plug my book *From Chicaza to Chickasaw*, which details the consequences of the slave trade for the southern Indians.

The Indians' New World by James Merrell. Merrell wrote this book in the late 1980s, yet it still stands as one of the best books about the formation of the historic coalescent societies, the Catawba, in particular, and their lives in the colonial world of the eighteenth century.

The House on Diamond Hill by Tiya Miles. This is a book about African slavery among the Cherokees. Miles reconstructs the story of the Vann family, a prominent, slaveholding Cherokee family. She writes beautifully, but she also opens up and answers numerous questions regarding African-Indian relations, Indians in the antebellum South, and so on.

Oh yes, *Hero, Hawk, and Open Hand*, edited by Townsend, is a magnificent book. It is the catalog from an Art Institute of Chicago exhibition of southern Indian objects, and the book has tons of stunning pictures. But the editor also solicited articles from leading authorities on various topics as well as some from Indigenous people. It's really a great book.

SSSL: What are some opportunities for new research in Native Southern Studies?

Howe: Thinking in terms of "Indigenous Studies" will open Native Southern scholars to new avenues of inquiry.

In my work as a Choctaw author, playwright, filmmaker, and scholar, I currently engage with the field of Indigenous Studies at the marrow of the bone. By that, I mean my scholarship and creative production seek to investigate the memories that we hold in our physical bodies; memories passed down for generations though kinship and fictive-kin memories, history; and the memories contained in sacred places such as Indigenous Earthworks in the Western Hemisphere.

At present, I'm involved in a four-year project, Indigenous Knowledge, Contemporary Performance, funded through the Social Sciences and Humanities Research Council of Canada that takes as its starting point the intersection of two research creation projects within Indigenous theater: first, embodied research on the recovery of Indigenous knowledge in the South, and, second, the development of trans-Indigenous dramaturgies. The project's potential contribution to Indigenous knowledge is immense because of its capacity to revitalize Native performance, long fixated on "the victim narrative," by turning to structural principles to Indigenous forms such as Earthworks.

Each of these related and overlapping projects centers around "test-case" performances under development and to be presented in 2015. The play

I'm writing for this project, *Sideshow Freaks and Circus Injuns*, coauthored with actress and playwright Monique Mojica, uses research from our family members' histories, memories passed down to dislodge the colonizer's gaze from the Indigenous *body*. We propose to use research from the relationship between the freak show, the ethnographic display of exotics—including Mojica's Kuna ancestors, some of them Albinos brought to the US and Canada in the early twentieth century—in sideshows, human zoos, circuses, and museums to investigate how the pornography of disability connects to the pornography of cultural diversity. The research-creation project asks, "How is memory held in our bodies? Where is it stored?" By embodying the experience of our immediate older generations in the South through embodied cultural memory, we explode the normalcy of the pornographer's gaze. In the traditions of southeastern ancestors, the Choctaw and the Rappahannock, we use mound building as a dramaturgical structure for our play. Hence, we are a multidisciplinary project. The creative and scholarly methods augment Indigenous epistemologies and Indigenous knowledge in the South.

Here's another example. I'm currently writing a new novel, *Memoir of a Choctaw in the Arab Revolt of 1917*, forthcoming in 2014. I was a Fulbright Scholar in 2010–2011 in Jordan during the Arab Spring. I began my research by asking questions. Where have Native missionaries been; when did they begin traveling abroad once they were converted to Christianity? So in my own work, I think of trans-Indigenous identity in the international arena.

Ethridge: It's wide open. I am interested in the early contact era, and that era is only now receiving much sustained scholarly attention. There are many, many questions that remain to be answered about the rise and fall of the precontact Mississippian world and the restructuring of life afterwards, including formation of the Cherokees, Creeks, Chickasaws, etc. The southern Indian experience in the Seven Years' War still needs more thorough scholarly treatment. We need a modern look at Removal for all the tribes of the South. Post-Removal studies still have much to be looked at. We also need more on twentieth- and twenty-first-century southern Indians.

The Native South, Performance, and Globalized Trans-Indigeneity: A Conversation with LeAnne Howe

Kirstin L. Squint / 2013

From Kirstin L. Squint, *LeAnne Howe at the Intersections of Southern and Native American Literature* (Baton Rouge: Louisiana State University Press, 2018), appendix. Reprinted by permission of Louisiana State University Press.

My second interview with Choctaw writer and professor LeAnne Howe was conducted on March 23, 2013, at the Dakota Nation's Mystic Lake Casino in Minneapolis, Minnesota, during the annual Native American Literature Symposium. Howe and I first met in 2008, when I interviewed her at the Society for the Study of Southern Literature's biennial conference in Williamsburg, Virginia. At that time, I was finishing my dissertation, one chapter of which examined spirituality in Howe's 2001 novel, *Shell Shaker*. That interview was eventually published in the journal *MELUS* (*Multi-Ethnic Literature of the United States*) in 2010.

Kirstin L. Squint: You were interviewed in the fall 2012 issue of the newsletter for the Society for the Study of Southern Literature in which you spoke at length about the burgeoning field of Native Southern Studies and about how you and other southeastern tribal peoples self-identify as both Native and southern. So, as an extension of that, do you consider your writing to be southern literature? Would you classify it that way?

LeAnne Howe: Yes. Absolutely.

KLS: Would you say that [the story] "Choctalking on Other Realities" is just as southern as *Shell Shaker*,[1] considering the difference in their settings, because they're coming from that same original space of people from Mississippi, or the place before Mississippi?

LH: Right.

KLS: So, the classification for you is always connected to land.

LH: Always. I have this collection of short stories coming out, *Choctalking on Other Realities: New and Selected Stories*. Years and years ago, I'd written a lot more on the Global South. In fact, there's "The Chaos of Angels." I don't see it as the Global South, but others may. I see it as the South, and there's a fight between a Choctaw woman and an African American woman, and she later morphs into Haiti because Choctaws were once exported as enslaved persons there in the 1700s, I believe. So, with the aid of the Chickasaws, a lot of our men were exported to work in the sugar plantations of what would become Haiti. So, I wrote this story, trying to intervene. It's set in Louisiana, in New Orleans, where we are everywhere, and we are nowhere. There's a line in *Shell Shaker* about that. But the South and southern studies had so long, has so long—this is a raging point for me—ignored us, in fact, excluded us. Natives from the Five Tribes could not be in this conversation because the South was about Black and white. Now, there are people like Eric [Gary Anderson][2] and a whole slew of really good scholars who are saying, "Well, perhaps we should think differently about this exclusion?" I'm appreciative of their work, but I'm really railing against that earlier southern literary tradition that wholly and completely left us out of the discourse, although I admit Faulkner invented southern Natives in narratives. So, when I met you at the conference,[3] I think I had said something to that effect. Craig Womack was there, I remember.

KLS: [And] Allison [Hedge Coke].[4]

LH: Allison was there. We were trying to intervene and say, "Look." And maybe the field has moved on, but I have remained unhappy about why it took so long to consider southeastern Natives in the discussions of the South. Natives have great allies in Eric Anderson and Annette Trefzer, to name only two. Historian Theda Perdue is another. Still it seems to me that our homelands establish us as original to the South, and for any discourse to exclude us is willful, intellectual amnesia. Rarely do scholars say, "Oh, I never knew there were Natives in the South." No, it's something much more dangerous. They say something like this: "Well, you are no longer in the South, so you can't be part of the discourse about the South. Alas." It's a willful desire to make us absent, to make us disappear. So many of the narratives with our beloved trickster rabbit come out of the South. It isn't African Americans who have excluded us though. It's typically been white southerners who have happily replaced Natives in the stories with their version of history. What should we call this purposeful act?

KLS: Genocide.[5]

LH: Yes, genocide.

KLS: Which is a word that is still not widely circulated in reference to Indian Removal and other similar US government-sanctioned acts.

LH: I know. That word is reserved for Jews and Jewish history, but it can and should also refer to American Indians.

KLS: I mean it's circulated in Native Studies, but it's not widely circulated in discourse about the South.

LH: That's right because, you know, it's this idea of "we didn't do anything wrong." And "You guys were interfering with progress." In *The Mascot Opera: A Minuet*, for instance, I made Andrew Jackson Andrea Jackson. His character would morph into this beautiful woman and then morph back to him as we are being replaced in the South. So, in that way I made him disappear. Kind of a tit for tat.

KLS: When did this come out? I haven't read it.

LH: A long time ago I wrote *The Mascot Opera: A Minuet* as a ten-minute play for Minneapolis Mixedblood Theatre, but it was either too complex—it was a musical after all—or they didn't like it. [*Laughs*] Whatever the case, they didn't produce it. I think probably in the next couple of years we'll do something about it again at Illinois because we have so many problems with the school's former mascot, Chief Illiniwek.[6] The point to all this is that I wrote it as a response to willful amnesia. *Shell Shaker* is a response to the South's willful amnesia. The fight for our lands and lands in Oklahoma continues. For example, when I was working on *Shell Shaker*, we were having our own warfare with our tribal chief.[7] He died in October 2011. He ended up going to prison. So tribal people are having to fight outsiders, and they're having to fight insiders, and you have to do it simultaneously. I was very active in Choctaws for Democracy, and so was Jacki Rand,[8] who was here yesterday at the conference. She presented on Mississippi Choctaws and violence against women, her current project. But Jacki and I and many others were a part of the Choctaws for Democracy, as was Scott Morrison, Doug Dry, Bob Burlison—there were hundreds of us during those years. At one meeting, I remember in Atoka, Oklahoma, there were nearly three hundred people gathered together concerned that some candidates running for chief were excluded from information they needed to run for office. The candidates couldn't get our tribe's voter registration records, so they could contact voters to ask for their vote. The tribe's lawyer, who was also the lawyer for the Chickasaws at that time, represented the tribe in order to ensure that Choctaws running for office could not get the registered voters list. The stakes of that election were so high—it was like a Third World election. But things only got worse. At that time, our former chief was also accused of raping women at work.

In writing *Shell Shaker*, I placed that stake in the ground in the eighteenth century in the Lower Mississippi Valley when things were tense for the southeastern tribes. In some ways, I think those events continued to haunt us into the twenty-first century. Because the Choctaws had a civil war that occurred because of Red Shoes in the eighteenth century, we had another kind of civil war in the 1990s. Choctaws for Democracy wanted to ensure that we could have a fair election. That's what I believe Choctaws for Democracy was all about. To this day, I think I pay a price for being part of the organization. Scott Morrison, a Choctaw lawyer and activist, is dead. I think Doug Dry went to work for the Muskogee Creeks; I'm not sure where he is working at this time.

KLS: Do you see Oklahoma as being culturally southern?

LH: Yes.

KLS: Can you talk about that a little bit? There are two things I'm thinking about: one, you've got the Five "Civilized Tribes" from the Southeast, and they are located in Oklahoma. In our last interview you talked about Choctaws taking the physical dirt and the land and the place names and all of that, with them, on the Trail of Tears.

LH: Everything about southeastern Oklahoma is southern: the foods, our heritage, and cultural and ceremonial lifeways. The "cult of grandmothers" is strong in Oklahoma among Natives and even non-Natives, another cultural lifeway that I argue comes from tribal people. What I mean is that everyone looks to the families' matriarchs for guidance, the oldest woman. Women control or run all kinds of businesses and community organizations in southeastern Oklahoma. Another example is the way southeastern Oklahomans speak. If you listen to the way in which we speak, it's an extremely southeastern accent. And I think I mentioned this before: southerners do not speak with a drawl because it's something they brought from, say, Ireland. I think it's because they were influenced by the Native pronunciation of vowels. We were talking yesterday with Gwen Westerman, who was raised in Oklahoma, and you know, she's Cherokee and Dakota. We were teasing her husband, and she said, "Say my name to him." And I said, "Gwee-in, Gwee-in." And it has multiple syllables, and he just laughed because he hasn't heard that so much because they live in Minnesota. We had this whole discussion on how our vowels and song-speak influenced southern speak. I know, I know, the linguists say otherwise. There's a scholar here from Ireland, Padraig Kirwan, and he and I laughed about how southern speak is supposed to be a derivation of Irish speech patterns. It's kind of funny when you think about it.

KLS: Earlier you were talking about the "Chaos of Angels" and the message that Grandmother had for the Choctaw woman was "You didn't get the joke. You responded with anger."

LH: "You responded with anger." Well, that character would be me. [*Laughs*] I'm the one who is always angry. But to get at that anger, I use humor. And so, Isaac in the novel [*Shell Shaker*] is the humorous character. He's very funny in the story and the way he comes at political issues, and yet, he's the character that must sacrifice himself. So, you know, in my new play, *Sideshow Freaks and Circus Injuns*, coauthored with Monique Mojica, I come out of Oklahoma, but the other characters I've created must go back to the mounds and crawl up through that cave in the mound and lose the wounds that centuries of colonialism have left on the body. My character is Panther Girl in this new play that we'll do in 2016. The long and the short of it is I'm trying to write myself healthy, perform myself healthy, by losing the wounds of the past three hundred years. I believe the art I create in my lifetime can heal the anger I carry. I'm speaking here also about historical grief and trauma.

KLS: You are an actress as well as a writer, professor, and critic. How do you see your experiences and worldview as a performer impacting your creative works? And what is the difference for you as an actress between writing drama or fiction and poetry?

LH: Well, I don't really think of myself as an actress.

KLS: You don't?

LH: I wish I was.

KLS: But you do perform, right?

LH: I'm a performer. Roxy [Gordon][9] and I in our early plays—we never thought of ourselves as actors: we were performers. And somebody else would always have to do the heavy acting in our plays.

KLS: Okay.

LH: So, Monique Mojica, who's my coauthor and coperformer, now she's a real actress because she can embody Shakespeare, she can embody, you know, characters on TV or [created] by other Native playwrights—I can't do that. I could never say I was an actress because I don't think I have the talent to do that. I do embody the South. I embody my homeland, both metaphorically and physically. I'm just this short, stocky Choctaw woman, who, you know, came up out of those mounds just like everybody else. But when I say things are about land—of course, I'm including more subjects that just "the land." I mean settler colonials want our bodies, our identity, our lifeblood, everything. But land is a thing I carry with me, just as my ancestors did when they carried dirt in their pockets from Nanih Waiya. By healing myself, metaphorically, we artists may end up healing the universe or spaces we inhabit. I'm trying to heal the space for my granddaughters. That they may grow into the healing is my highest desire for them. This all sounds like a lot of malarkey, I know. But there it is.

KLS: You mentioned in the *SSSL Newsletter* interview, in regards to *Sideshow Freaks and Circus Injuns*, that you saw this work as revitalizing Native performance. How do you see that happening?

LH: Of course, *Indian Radio Days* is not that kind of play, and *Big Pow-Wow* was set again at Nanih Waiya with the old ghost, a bone picker, which is an earlier play. Roxy and I were working through the past. We were reimagining an Indigenous literary tradition and an Indigenous performance tradition. I've written a paper that will probably be out this year on the Bird Mound at Poverty Point in Louisiana, how it was created in three months, which mirrors the three months' gestation for a red-tailed hawk. But *Sideshow Freaks and Circus Injuns* is a different animal, pun intended. It reveals, I think, a different meaning of Indigenous performance.

KLS: Can you talk more about the relationship between Bird Mound and performance?

LH: Red-tailed hawks embody special meanings for southeastern Natives, especially Choctaws. The red-tailed hawk is a solar bird, one of power and strength, and the tail feathers are bright red in sunlight. Red signifies lifeblood and is sometimes a powerful metaphor for war. These predator birds mate over a period of a few days in late winter or early spring. By March, the female lays her eggs, one every other day; two eggs in a nest can take up to four days to be laid. The incubation period for hawk eggs is typically thirty-five days. It generally takes another four days for the small nestlings to hatch out of their shells. Once out of their shells, the nestlings will spend another forty-six days or so in the nest before the baby birds begin to leave on short flights. The total time needed to create a red-tailed hawk, from mating to a fledgling leaving the nest, is approximately ninety days. Three months. Therefore, it would seem that Bird Mound at Poverty Point is possibly a performance mound that embodies the story of the red-tailed hawk from conception to first flight—the story of its creation. What were our ancestors trying to say in that three months' building period? It was a performance of creation. We're trying to show through this process of embodiment, of embodying land, that story that comes up out of land. That bird mound is indeed influential to Choctaw people today because the red-tailed hawk is emblematic of our power as a group. That mound is five thousand years old, and knowing the mound's interaction with our culture is pretty remarkable. That southeastern embodiment, of knowing ourselves connected to the land, still affects me as an artist. I'm still working through not only our mounds, but understanding the performative aspect of many mounds. Hopefully, that "knowing" will come out in the play *Sideshow Freaks and Circus Injuns*. These days Native performers and writers are asking twenty-first-century questions. No longer are we content to write a victim's narrative. In *Sideshow*, we're trying to create a performance on the land, something our ancestors were trying to create five thousand years ago. Oh dear, more hubris, I know, I know.

KLS: And so, to be dislocated, or disenfranchised, from the land means losing an essential part of your lifeways.

LH: Right.

KLS: You engage with that land. It's part of the story, but it's also a part of the body.

LH: It's part of the body. And it's part of the Native physical and political landscape. They've just found that the Rappahannock had an ancient mound. So what we are doing is imagining a similar kind of process with this play, performing at mound sites all across Native North America. And it crosses many generations. My great aunt joined the circus in the late 1920s and "played Indian." It's my own narrative intertwined with many others from southeastern Oklahoma. Monique's writing about her family's experience in the circus. There are multiple collisions that make this play possible. My work is about land and all of the manifestations that have to do with "southeastern-ness."

KLS: We keep coming back to this theme. I'm really excited to hear you talking about this. This is what I sort of suspected, and you've said it in other ways.

LH: And "southeastern-ness" continues to influence my future work. We have a gang of people at work with us to help articulate the work through embodied performance, Chickasaw, Choctaw artists from Oklahoma, along with First Nations artists. Can we heal ourselves? Can we be healed through art? I think we can. We're hopeful that, once the work is up, we can begin teaching from it—about historical grief and trauma. Then we'll see if the process is helpful. I hope. I hope.

KLS: I read in your blog that you did [the short story] "Choctalking on Other Realities" as a one-woman show a couple of years ago. I'm curious how that text changed when you changed form. Or did it? Or what did it mean to you?

LH: I didn't change the text. I was working with a filmmaker, Jim Fortier, who created nine short films, to enhance the visualization of a one-woman show. There are film cues that come up, and you'll see a child's feet, for instance, that morphs into a closet that morphs into the riot in Jerusalem, in East Jerusalem, that happened when I was there, which was during the Intifada. The story circles back to the 1960s when African Americans were changing and calling for civil rights, and American Indians were doing similarly. During the show, nine short film segues flanked that performance. They served to bring the audience back into the restaurant, to the characters of those three women in the narrative that were Jewish, African American, and Choctaw. I played all the parts. That's the only difference.

KLS: During the 2010–2011 academic year, you were a Fulbright Scholar in Amman, Jordan. What is it about Jordan and its culture that attract you, and more broadly, how did you become interested in the Middle East?

LH: Tribes. I spent a lot of time with tribes in 1992 and 1993. I lived in Jordan from 1993 to 1994. The first time I went to the Middle East I was on a study tour in 1992, and we went to Jordan and the occupied territories which included Gaza. When we went to live in Jordan in 1993, I realized there were literally hundreds of tribes there. Jordanians are extremely tribal. At that time social justice was meted out by judges within these tribes that cooperated with one another. For instance, someone had shot a man from a different tribe, so the judges in the tribes meted out justice. All the members of the offending tribe, whose member shot someone from the other tribe, had to leave town for fifteen years. I repeat: every member of that tribe had to pack up and leave town for fifteen years. It only seemed fair if you think about it. That the punishment is communal has a chilling effect on mayhem in the future. Tribes and tribalism in the Middle East fascinated me. Some things, lifeways, just made sense to me. So, I fell in the love with the people and the deserts. They took us into their homes and lands and hosted us, and I responded. It was call and response. I had the piece "Choctalking on Other Realities," and when I went back to Jordan as a Fulbright Scholar, I just happened to be there during the Arab Spring, when the Middle East erupted. Hence, a new book. My Choctaw character goes to Bilaad ash Sham in 1913 and stays through the Arab Revolt. He gives up Christianity and becomes something newly created.

KLS: He's a missionary, right?

LH: [*Laughs*] Right, at first he is. But he gives it up for a newly created life.

KLS: In the SSSL interview, you said that you were trying to birth a new form of trans-Indigenous novel. Can you talk about what that process is like and maybe how it is similar to or departs from your approaches in *Shell Shaker* and *Miko Kings*?

LH: Oh, this new book is a completely different animal, and let me just say, I realize my new work could be a ginormous failure.

KLS: Isn't that always true in a creative work, though? You're going out on a limb?

LH: Yes, but I've always thought that Natives are/were creating larger frames in their narratives. At least this is how I read American Indian, Indigenous, literature—that it is, indeed, a tribalography.[10] So, what does that really mean in praxis? I'm interested in answering that question. This new "novel"—if it works—will have film, memoir, fiction, songs, and imagery in an e-book format. I'm grabbing all the things that I work in, including poetry and song and writing and filming and performing, in a text. And it is trans-Indigenous and trans-genre. The epilogue will be interviews with the descendants of some of the Arabs that fought in that revolt. They will tell their own story.

KLS: But you know what? I'm just curious, as someone who thinks about your work a lot—

LH: Oh, God, I can't imagine that. Sounds terrible, is it?!

KLS: Ha! Not in the least. One of the amazing things about *Shell Shaker* is how you move between centuries, and it pulls together some very diverse cultural and temporal issues. And you have some mixed media in *Miko Kings*, right? If you look at your work in an arc, can you see this novel as a progression of things you've tried? I realize it's a very new form that you're talking about by using digital media in a way that people still really aren't doing.

LH: *His Last Game* was a film, and it was incorporated into the story.[11]

KLS: You had actual newspaper clippings too.

LH: Yes, newspaper clippings. And Ezol is traveling across time. She is the cosmos, in some ways. She's really telling a story of our math. She's really talking poetry. She also appears in *His Last Game* in the book. The book opens with, "This is a film. This is a book. This is a story." And so I do see this as a progression that technology allows me to make. But I don't believe that Natives separate by genre, at least not in the storytelling, so it feels right to be able to do the work. But, you know, I know a lot of people who think that this is just outrageous. And my own graduate students are like, "Hmmm. But it's a text, right?"

KLS: Do you anticipate going in a similar direction after this book?

LH: Yeah, but I don't know what it is yet. We were talking about this because I want to know where we're going as a field. Where are we going as a field? I want to be a part of that conversation, but I'm not quite sure what the conversation will be.

KLS: So we were talking about the form as being the new element.

LH: Again, it could be failure. [*Laughs*]

KLS: I understand. But then you have also said "a new form of trans-Indigenous novel." Is that something that already exists? Are you thinking of that in a line like *Almanac of the Dead*? I just mean the trans-Indigenous part.

LH: No, I didn't invent trans-Indigenous because, you know, that's what Chad Allen talks about.[12] I'm saying that this work is new because by going across the ocean it links tribes in the East and tribes in the West.

KLS: As opposed to all descendants of people of the Americas.

LH: Right. You know, Leslie [Marmon Silko] in [her novel] *Almanac of the Dead* goes to Asia.

KLS: And there's the African connection.

LH: Right, she goes east, Africa, Mexico. Her novel is situating and is pivoting in this way, between North-South-East-West. So, in that way, perhaps I'm in conversation with what Leslie Silko was doing twenty years ago.

KLS: You've also written about connections—and we've already talked about this a little bit—between Native Americans and Palestinians, with a character in "Choctalking on Other Realities" claiming that Oklahoma was the first Israel. How do you see Indigenous American issues intersecting with Palestinian issues, and what draws you to this particular example as opposed to other examples of settler colonialism around the globe?

LH: Land. And it was something that I saw firsthand. I saw it for myself. They were fighting over dispossession of one people for another group of people. This is just something that I saw, and I could make sense of in my writing.

KLS: So much of your writing is meticulously researched and contains representations of historical figures and events. What do you feel is the relationship between fiction and history in your work? We just had a conversation today about actual historical events in relation to *Shell Shaker* and Choctaws for Democracy.

LH: I see history as story that historians tell. Yesterday I was just with two historians on the ethics panel. We had two historians at our table, and we come at story in very different ways. Jacki [Rand][13] said, "Well, history has to be objective." I think, "Is that really true though?" I don't think I'm telling an objective story, so I guess that is one big difference. I'm telling a true story. Whether it's fiction or history. It's true that the world is created in a novel. In *Miko Kings*, the history of Oklahoma as Indian Territory and the baseball games were something that mainstream people in the late twentieth century had never heard of. Crash Parr who is a Cherokee from Oklahoma—from Tulsa—had written a lot on baseball's sandlots. He had given me a lot of research he had gathered. When I began to look at the newspaper archives, my God, Indians playing baseball in Indian Territory was just everywhere. But people had totally forgotten about it, didn't know it, couldn't remember. A lot of the work that I *think* I do is recovering stories that are there. The story wants to be told. In my writer's hands the story must have a twist. And here's the thing: I don't think I seek the stories out. The story looms somewhere in the ether and finds me. Certainly, this missionary character in my new novel goes to the Middle East. It's a story that wants to be told. I'm not sure I would have chosen it, even though I have loved living in Jordan. But I'm happy to be writing it. In that way, I am like a historian, only different.

KLS: In *Miko Kings* there is this newspaper image—it's the front-page story on the San Francisco earthquake. What Ezol comments on is related to Choctaws in the community, and it's an interesting juxtaposition. That headline is just blaring "San Francisco Earthquake," and she's talking about this other history that is important and relevant to her experience and her uncle's experience. How do you manage to negotiate tensions between personal and/or individual histories and public or dominant cultural memories of history? Do you feel like you're trying to negotiate that?

LH: Yes. I tell you whom I rely on as one of my mentors, although he probably doesn't know it. Raymond Fogelson, an emeritus professor at the University of Chicago, wrote a wonderful paper on the ethnohistory of events and nonevents. The San Francisco earthquake was an epitomizing event, especially for the dominant culture, but it wasn't to folks in Oklahoma, so theoretically, I relied on his work to help me negotiate the questions I had about certain events in *Miko Kings*. Ray has been a mentor to about a million graduate students at the University of Chicago, and he's also been a mentor to American Indians. Okay, a million may be an exaggeration! Ray worked with Will West Long when he was a young scholar. Will West Long was a medicine person in North Carolina, Eastern Band of Cherokee Indians. I quote Ray in "The Story of America: A Tribalography." In my work, I think I'm trying to recover southeastern Indian ways of being. Maybe that also comes from my grandparents because they were commenting and reading the paper twice a day, they listened to the radio every morning, they talked to the birds and small animals living in the trees around their house, they were interested in tribal things and spirits, and they also sat with the dead when called upon for funerals. Their lives were a tribalography in which they were adding to their experiences.

KLS: At this conference, they put me on a parody panel. I hadn't considered that I was writing about parody when I submitted my abstract, even though the paper is on Hollywood Indians and other simulations in your work. So I've been thinking about humor, and you've already talked a bit today about the way that you use humor as a coping mechanism. This morning I had a chance to read some of the introduction to *Seeing Red*,[14] the section about humor and trickster figures and dealing with these dominant cultural narratives about Indians. Can you just talk some more about the way that you use humor and satire and parody? Is it primarily a coping mechanism? Do you also see it coming out of a trickster tradition?

LH: You should talk to my colleague Harvey about that. Harvey Markowitz worked with the Lakota. He speaks Lakota. He wrote that section on humor in *Seeing Red: Hollywood's Pixeled Skins*. My relatives, my family, are, among other things, a bunch of jokers. Everybody was always joking. In fact, I joke a lot and sometimes my jokes fall flat. My editor, for instance, doesn't see humor in my work especially when I am a year late for deadlines.

KLS: [*Laughs*]

LH: They're very earnest people, editors. Seriously, I'm irreverent. I use vulgar language in my stories because it makes me laugh. I'm my own audience, I guess. I'm probably better at irony than straight-out humor. But the jokes in *Indian Radio Days* are pretty funny.

KLS: I was looking at my paper last night and laughing out loud at the quotes that I had pulled out of the play because they're just so funny. And I realized I had couched some of it in this very serious, critical perspective. But, you know, "Red Woman Tobacco" is not that far off from "Red Man Tobacco" or "Cheap Cherokee/Jeep Cherokee."

LH: Big Chief and Little Brave condoms.[15]

KLS: It is funny.

LH: Yeah, but when we went to the Smithsonian to perform *Indian Radio Days*, we'd have an all-white audience, and they didn't laugh at all. Some humor doesn't translate, but we'd go to Indian communities to perform and people would fall out of their chairs. They just fell out. Men, women, children laughing. You know, "what plays in New York won't play in Poughkeepsie." Mainstream audiences at that time didn't feel they could laugh because we were supposed to be the "stoic Indians."

KLS: I guess maybe we're getting past those cultural assumptions. I showed that clip to my students last semester of you on the *Daily Show* talking about the Chief Illiniwek controversy. This was after we had read *Shell Shaker*, so they had some contextualization, and when you gave Aasif Mandvi an "Indian Burn," one of my students couldn't quit laughing. He said, "I can't believe LeAnne Howe would do that."

LH: Why do I know how to do that? [*Laughs*] Aasif said, "Give me the Indian Burn." [*Makes Indian Burn sound effect.*] He said, "Oh, that really hurt!" I said, "Why do both of us know what that is?" And we laughed. Yeah, wasn't that wild?

KS: Yeah.

LH: Indians are pretty damn funny. I think it is a coping mechanism, but we're also funny people. It's surprising there are not more Native stand-up comedians. In my next life.

Notes

1. The short story "Choctalking on Other Realities" [later the title of Howe's 2013 volume] is set in both Oklahoma and Israel during the twentieth century, whereas *Shell Shaker* takes place in the lower Mississippi Valley during the eighteenth century and moves between Oklahoma and Mississippi in the twentieth century. [Notes with this interview are from the original publication except for number 10. Ellipses in the interview indicate text omitted for this volume. Content insertions made for this volume in both the interview and notes are in brackets.—Ed.]

2. Eric Gary Anderson, author of *American Indian Literature and the Southwest: Contexts and Dispositions,* as well as numerous articles on the intersection of Native American and southern literary studies.

3. Howe is referring to our first interview at the 2008 Society for the Study of Southern Literature biennial conference in Williamsburg, Virginia, where she was an invited speaker.

4. Allison Hedge Coke [is an American poet and editor of Indigenous and European heritage who teaches at the University of California, Riverside].

5. What Howe is referring to here is probably best described as "discursive genocide," a term [Michelle H.] Raheja uses [in *Reservation Reelism: Redfacing, Visual Sovereignty, and Representations of Native Americans in Film*] to describe how "Indigenous peoples had been written out of the present and the future of the United States" (15). It is also useful to consider the United Nations' complex definition of genocide. Article 2 of the Convention on the Prevention and Punishment of the Crime of Genocide (1948) defines genocide as "any of the following acts with intent to destroy, in whole or in part, a national, ethnical, racial, or religious group, as such: killing members of the group; causing serious bodily or mental harm to members of the group; deliberately inflicting on the group conditions of life calculated to bring about its physical destruction in whole or in part; imposing measures intended to prevent births within the group; [and] forcibly transferring children of the group to another group" (Office of the UN Special Advisor on the Prevention of Genocide).

6. The controversy surrounding the University of Illinois's decision to remove Chief Illiniwek as mascot in 2007 has continued to have traumatic implications for Native Americans on campus. In her 2012 interview in the *Society for the Study of Southern Literature Newsletter,* Howe describes bomb threats and death threats received by the

faculty of the American Indian Studies program, as recently as 2011. Chief Illiniwek is still the university's unofficial mascot.

7. Hollis E. Roberts.

8. Jacki Thompson Rand, associate professor of history at the University of Iowa.

9. Roxy Gordon, with whom Howe coauthored *Big PowWow* and *Indian Radio Days*.

10. See the introduction and conclusion of this volume for definitions and discussions of tribalography.—Ed.

11. The conversation now shifts to the use of mixed media in *Miko Kings*.

12. Author of *Trans-Indigenous: Methodologies for Global Native Literary Studies* (2012).

13. Jacki [Thompson] Rand [is associate professor of history and coordinator of Native American and Indigenous studies at the University of Iowa].

14. *Seeing Red: Hollywood's Pixeled Skins—American Indians and Film* (2013).

15. [From satirical ads written and performed in *Indian Radio Days* for] "Straight Arrow Brand Condoms."

Tonto, *The Lone Ranger*, and Indians in Film

Craig Chamberlain / 2013

From University of Illinois News Bureau, July 3, 2013. Reprinted by permission of Craig Chamberlain, University of Illinois News Bureau.

LeAnne Howe, a professor of American Indian Studies, is a coeditor of a recently published collection of thirty-six reviews on nearly a century of films that have portrayed Native Americans.

With the opening of *The Lone Ranger* in theaters July 3, most of the buzz is not about the title character but about Tonto, his Comanche sidekick, played by Johnny Depp in extravagant face paint and with a bird for a headdress. Tonto is not just any American Indian character, says LeAnne Howe, a coeditor of a recently published collection of thirty-six reviews on nearly a century of films that have portrayed Native Americans. Tonto was the only on-screen hero American Indians had growing up in the 1950s, says Howe, a Choctaw and a professor of American Indian Studies, English, and theater at Illinois. Howe spoke with News Bureau social sciences editor Craig Chamberlain about Tonto and the history of Indians on screen.

Craig Chamberlain: It's easy to think that many American Indians have taken one look at Johnny Depp as Tonto in trailers for this movie and dismissed the portrayal as the worst kind of stereotype. But the actor has been adopted by the Comanche Nation, which you note is no small thing. What's going on here?
LeAnne Howe: One word: Hollywood.
Seriously, American Indians have a long and complicated relationship with Hollywood films. Over the last hundred years, images of American Indians have populated Hollywood films so much so that when viewers see

an Indian in a headdress, they recognize the story as American. As early as 1908, real American Indians worked as consultants and advisers to film-makers—supposedly to make the storyline more authentic. For example, Lillian St. Cyr and James Youngdeer, enrolled members of the Nebraska Ho-Chunk Tribe, embraced moviemaking and worked as technical advisers for D. W. Griffith's *Indian Runner's Romance* (1909) and other films. A former chief of the Abenaki Tribe, actor Elijah Tahamont, stage name Dark Cloud, was another early technical adviser for such films as *The Song of the Wild-wood Flute* (1910).

The latest updating of *The Lone Ranger* has cultural advisers as well, from the Comanche Nation. The film's portrayal of Tonto is a continuation of a Hollywood tradition, complete with the stereotypical bare-chested warrior in a feathered headdress. What makes this film unique for moviegoers is that Johnny Depp was officially adopted into the Comanche Nation in May 2012, in a ceremony in Lawton, Oklahoma. It is a case where art becomes life. Depp plays a Comanche and is then adopted by respected Comanche elder LaDonna Harris, founder of Americans for Indian Opportunity.

As Harris's adopted son, Depp is an honorary member of the tribe, but not an enrolled citizen. The adoption ceremony that honored Depp is more than just recognition; it's a reciprocal relationship between obligated parties. Depp gave gifts to those in attendance as a sign of respect. In return, he'll be received as a family member within the Comanche Nation. Over the centuries, Native Americans have adopted many non-Indians into their tribes, including President Obama, adopted into the Crow Nation in 2008.

Chamberlain: What's different about the Tonto character in past radio, TV, and film compared to many other Indian portrayals? Why was he such a hero?

Howe: Perhaps Tonto's longevity is part of what sets him above other Native American characters in film or television. Tonto emerged in 1936 on the radio and evolved through many script transformations until the television series *The Lone Ranger* solidified the character. Tonto was played by Mohawk actor Jay Silverheels, who had his own fan club and newsletter titled *The Tom Tom*. For American Indians my age, Silverheels was the only Native actor we would ever see on television. Imagine growing up in America and never seeing a white actor on television—except one. So, of course, Tonto was a heroic character for us.

Chamberlain: You encouraged those writing the film reviews for your book to be funny and play with stereotypes. To reinforce that, your rating system for the thirty-six films employs tomahawks for thumbs down and feathers for thumbs up. Why this approach? And how might this be key for Depp and the new movie, if done right?

Howe: Coeditors Harvey Markowitz, Denise Cummings, and I wanted a general audience to find humor in the way American Indians are represented in film. Our rating system and the reviews in *Seeing Red: Hollywood's Pixeled Skins* poke fun at the genre and make the discussion of ugly stereotypes livelier. Humor is a way to get at painful aspects of racism depicted in films such as *She Wore a Yellow Ribbon* (1949) or *Broken Arrow* (1950). I suspect *The Lone Ranger* has to be humorous for some of the same reasons. Besides, the same team of Gore Verbinski and Jerry Bruckheimer created the *Pirates of the Caribbean* series.

Chamberlain: Why have Indians been such a key part of American movies—even, you say, when they're not actually in them?

Howe: Conquest is an American master narrative; it permeates our culture. In the film *Independence Day* (1996), the storyline is about aliens landing on Earth and attempting to wipe out all Indigenous life. Sound familiar? Aliens want to harvest all the planet's resources. Ditto. The film references Europeans' hunger for other lands and resources; only this time the Indigenous people are not going to lose it, as Native Americans did, to aliens. When President Thomas Whitmore, played by Bill Pullman, gives that rousing speech about not going quietly into that good night, American audiences cheered in theaters around the country. The film simultaneously twins the history of Native Americans with American exceptionalism, and the "Indians," or rather human beings, win.

Chamberlain: Do you have one or two movies, from among those in the book, which you'd suggest as the worst in their portrayals of Indians? And one or two that are must-sees?

Howe: So glad you asked. *A Man Called Horse* (1970) is a four-tomahawks-down film. Along with *Tell Them Willie Boy Is Here* (1969). Ugh! But *The Unforgiven* (1960), starring Audrey Hepburn as a Kiowa Indian, is a must-see.

"Stories of the Marvelous": An Interview with LeAnne Howe

Erin Regan / 2013

From *Superstition Review*, Issue 12 (Fall 2013). Reprinted by permission of *Superstition Review*.

LeAnne Howe is the author of novels, plays, essays, screenplays, and poetry. Her latest book, *Choctalking on Other Realities* (Aunt Lute Books, 2013), is a memoir about her travels abroad. She is coeditor of *Seeing Red: Hollywood's Pixeled Skins—American Indians and Film* (Michigan State University Press, 2013). An enrolled citizen of the Choctaw Nation of Oklahoma, she has won multiple national and international awards including the 2012 USA Artist Ford Fellowship, a $50,000 award from United States Artists. She's a professor in the MFA program and American Indian Studies and affiliated faculty in the Theatre Department at the University of Illinois.

This interview was conducted via email by Interview Editor Erin Regan. Of the process she said, "I first came across LeAnne Howe's book of poetry *Evidence of Red* and fell in love with her wit and playfulness with literary conventions. Her spirit is surely reflected here." In this interview, Howe discusses her use of humor, the freedom of other creative forms, and the metaphysical power of language.

Superstition Review: You often use humor in your writing. What is your approach to incorporating humor in stories about the disenfranchisement and abuse of Native Americans?

LeAnne Howe: Humor defuses pain. Humor gives the narrators in my stories agency to tilt at the ever-whirling windmills of colonization. Humor opens a window on historic pain and trauma that American Indians dealt with at the hands of the federal government. Loss of land, loss of dignity, loss of identity, and of course the loss of a brother or sister, parent—which in my great-grandmother's era was a common event. As I think back to my early childhood, I can say that I was raised around a bunch of jokers. All Indians, and they were always pointing out little ironies. My humor these days tends toward irony, but often falls flat in the classroom. My students are not familiar with irony or thinking about the historical past as having anything to do with them.

SR: In *Miko Kings*, the principal of the Hampton Normal School for Blacks and Indians tells Hope Little Leader, "by cultivating you wild Indians . . . we tame the land" [ellipsis in original]. In what ways is the subjugation of American Indians tied to the exploitation of land?

LH: I believe American Indians are seen as the flora and fauna, another reason that the Bureau of Indian Affairs is located squarely within the Department of the Interior and maintained by the Secretary of the Interior. What would people say if there were such a thing as the Bureau of African American Affairs and it was located within the Department of the Interior? The Department of the Interior has oversight over land management, fish and game, wildlife, *and* American Indians. So, in that way, taming Indians is like taming the land, the reason that I wrote that section in *Miko Kings*.

SR: *Evidence of Red* features poetry, prose, and dramatic script. How did you decide to use all of these forms in one collection?

LH: I'm not exactly sure how it happened. When I was writing the poems, I was thinking about the book as a whole piece of cloth and realized that it would be more colorful with different genres included. I'm extremely lucky that the editor of the Earthworks series, Janet McAdams, allowed me to do this. Currently, I'm working on a new collection of poems, and right now it's all poetry. Perhaps, a better answer to this genre-switching thing that I often do—*Choctalking*'s format is a bit funky, too—is that I have a short attention span. I'll be writing along and think, "Hum, maybe this isn't a poem, perhaps it's a screenplay." Lately, I'm writing song lyrics that I originally thought were poems. I suspect I'm going to find out that my song lyrics stink and go back to writing lyrical poems.

SR: In *Evidence of Red*, you use the motifs of Indian Mascot and Noble Savage to challenge the character tropes of American Indians in the media. How has popular culture contributed to the suppression of realistic American Indian narratives? What is your approach to writing more realistic representations?

LH: There are no other images of American Indians in popular culture except those of a bare-chested brave in a feathered headdress, or the Indian maiden offering a box of Land O'Lakes butter to presumably settler colonials who've just landed on the shores of Gitche Gumee, Lake Superior. I wrote ten-second commercials for *Indian Radio Days* that I coauthored with Roxy Gordon about "Cheap Cherokees" and "Red Woman Chewing Tobacco." After WagonBurner Theatre Troop was formed in 1993, we, the members of the dramatic troupe, wrote more commercials about Native products such as these:

> *"Try new Straight Arrow Brand Condoms for the utmost in prophylactic protection. Straight Arrow Brand condoms are made from the intestines of buffalo and are naturally lubricated. They come in three sizes: Big Chief, Bad Warrior, and Little Brave. You're always prepared to defend yourself and your partner with Straight Arrow Brand Condoms."*
>
> *"Mom, do you ever get that not so fresh feeling?" "Why, yes daughter, and when I do I reach for new Moontime Organic Tampons. They're made from the cattails which grow by rivers and ponds and were used by Native American women when they were also feeling not-so-fresh. Here, try Moontime Organic Tampons." "Thanks, Mom."*

So, we're back to the Indian humor. In the case of *Indian Radio Days*, it diffuses pain of stereotypes.

SR: According to your biography in *Shell Shaker*, you have worked as a waitress, a factory worker making stems for plastic champagne glasses, and a journalist. How have your previous jobs influenced your work as a writer? Do you feel like writers with more varied experiences have a richer palette?

LH: Working in all kinds of situations helps a writer make sense of the world. At least it did for me. But fewer and fewer writers haven't worked outside of a university or college environment. Of course, there are the writers who've attended law schools. That makes sense because law school teaches how to manipulate language. But I'm not sure whether doing a lot of different kinds of work is a good thing or not. We have quite a few young writers who've gone from being undergraduates to an MFA program and now are publishing their four and fifth novels. So who can say? I worked in all kinds of professions and crappy jobs. But that doesn't mean everyone else should.

SR: You are also a filmmaker and playwright. What do you most enjoy about performance arts? In what ways do those mediums enhance a written text?

LH: I like performing in a theater troupe, in the classroom, or during a reading. For years I was so shy and then *whamo*, I came out of the performance closet and met a new self onstage. I do think that reading aloud, or performing one's own work, is very helpful to the writing process. You can hear the voices you are creating, see the scenes you've created, and where the text falters.

SR: Will you describe what it means to perform in the classroom? Do you encourage your students to perform?

LH: I think most really good teachers, or professors, prepare for their classes as any writer/performer does. You write and then learn your lines, you draw your students into the performance or lecture just as any performer does, and you write a conclusion to the day's performance or lesson just as any performer does. Yes, I have my students "perform" in class in a variety of ways. Sometimes I ask them to collaborate and put their lessons into a play format. Or recently I asked my students to make a short film and then talk about it. They wrote action scenes that reinforced the class discussions. Learning is supposed to be fun, funny, dramatic, and full of irony. A performance.

SR: You use the voice of Ezol Day to experiment with time in the novel *Miko Kings*. Her spirit travels from 1907 to tell Lena, the modern-day narrator, the Miko Kings' story. What freedoms did you find when you began to play with time?

LH: I think the way I come at a story has always been from thinking about the past—American Indian history, my family's history, my tribe's history—and how the present and future are shaped by the past. Put another way, I am certain that we humans live in past, present, and future all at the same time. It's probably the reason I am attracted to quantum physics; I read a great many physicists as I was writing *Miko Kings: An Indian Baseball Story*.

SR: That's fascinating. Would you expand on your research process for *Miko Kings*?

LH: I spent five years researching and writing *Miko Kings: An Indian Baseball Story*. I was lucky and found an Oklahoma baseball historian named Crash Parr, a Cherokee from Tulsa, Oklahoma. He was so helpful to me in my process and gave me copies of newspaper clippings that he had from the 1900s through about 1926, something like that. I read those newspaper clippings and other newspapers. I also conducted fieldwork, interviewing Choctaws and other southeastern Indian ball players at the eleven tribal tournaments that take place each summer in Oklahoma. I read a lot of chaos theory. The book's subtext is chaos and how Natives interact with the chaos through playing ball games.

SR: Ezol uses the Choctaw language to explain the fluidity of time in *Miko Kings*: "The laws of physics do not distinguish between past and present.

Neither does the Choctaw language, at least not in the way that English does." Would you explain how you use language to manipulate time in your fiction?

LH: Choctaw doesn't distinguish between past, present, and future tenses, not in the same way English does. So I theorized that was another reason we viewed time differently from English speakers.

SR: Does writing primarily in English limit you?

LH: Not yet.

SR: The color red plays a central role in several of your works—it represents the earth, war, and blood sacrifice. How do you incorporate symbols, such as color, in your writing?

LH: Oklahoma is a Choctaw word; it means home of the red people. Okla = people, homa, or humma = red. Our tribe was broken into two divisions, white and red. These are metaphors, of course, but at the same time red and white represent our tribal colors today. It is also very easy to think about one's life in terms of red and white. White being a color all humans move into as we age. White is for peace and tranquility. Red is a passionate color, and early in our lives most of us live a passionate life. And for women, red holds a particularly strong image in our lives.

SR: Your novel *Shell Shaker* does not rely on a single protagonist's voice but instead is told through many characters. What inspired you to include so many narrators in the story, and how does that technique reinforce the theme of community in the novel?

LH: As I have said before, I grew up in a house of women, and in my family, there were many speakers all telling the same story from different points of view. I don't think I would be very good at writing a story from one POV. It just doesn't feel right for me—as a writer. In all my novels, there are multiple points of view from a variety of characters. Many characters in different settings tell the story in my current novel project. The novel takes place in Allen, Oklahoma, and Bilaad ash Sham in 1917 and today, 2011. However, in the memoir *Choctalking on Other Realities*, the POV is mine.

SR: Your works are populated by such powerful women. As I was reading *Shell Shaker*, I started hearing the Billy women's voices during other parts of my day. What is your process for developing these characters? Do their voices come to you first?

LH: Yes. I often hear them, just a word or two at first, but I'm compelled by their voice. Then I go to work on who they are, what they look like, and build outward. In terms of Grandmother of Birds, an ancient relative in *Shell*

Shaker, I saw an image of her—in, of all places, a fashion magazine. The picture didn't have anything to do with Choctaws, or American Indians, but for some reason her character began to cook after I saw the image.

SR: In your newest collection, *Choctalking on Other Realities*, you frame your stories with theoretical essays that you have termed "tribalography." Please describe your goal with these essays and how you came to identify them as tribalography.

LH: In the memoir *Choctalking on Other Realities*, I'm trying to show how one thing leads to another and is connected in the memories we embody the rest of our lives. I'm also trying to show what tribalography is for American Indians, how we embody our particular tribal histories as well. I was born in Edmond, Oklahoma, in a home for unwed Indian mothers. After five days, my adopted Cherokee mother came for me, and we traveled together to my Cherokee grandmother's house, yet I am wholly Choctaw. If it seems like a contradiction, it is. But that is the basis for all stories.

SR: You've also described *Choctalking on Other Realities* as "three parts memoir, one part tragedy, one part absurdist fiction, and one part 'marvelous realism.'" Would you explain how you came to identify the work in that way? How do these genres intersect?

LH: I am not sure that there are such things as genres when writers sit down to write. Oh, perhaps I better speak for myself—I like how one frame or structure leads to another. In *Choctalking*, I've woven a text from all these strands called "genres." There is poetry, prose, a screenplay, memoir, and "marvelous realism," or stories of the marvelous that most American Indians grow up with.

SR: What does your writing space look like?

LH: Messy. Very messy. I have a room with a view, lots of bright colors, purple walls, Native blankets, pillows, and papers and books scattered everywhere. I have two cats that have their beds on either side of a long writing desk in my office. I type, they sleep. When I read aloud and I think it's pretty good, they purr. Or stretch a paw in my direction. When it's bad, they ignore me. It's a good life.

It's about Story

Gina Caison / 2016

From *About South Podcast*, Season 1, Episode 6 (August 11, 2016). Printed by permission of Gina Caison and Kelly R. Vines. The interview has been edited for content for this volume.

Gina Caison: Happy Friday, everyone! We're happy to bring you the sixth episode of *About South,* and this week we are talking about the Native South with LeAnne Howe and Kirstin Squint. We were able to have this conversation when we attended the Faulkner and Yoknapatawpha Conference in Oxford, Mississippi, this summer. This year's topic was on Faulkner and the Native South. We were delighted to get the chance to sit down with Professor Howe and Professor Squint and discuss their work and what we might mean by something now called "the Native South." Choctaw author LeAnne Howe is the Eidson Distinguished Professor in American Literature at the University of Georgia. She has won numerous awards, including the Lifetime Achievement Award from the Native Writers' Circle of the Americas, and in 2014 she received the Modern Language Association's inaugural prize for Studies in Native American Literatures, Cultures, and Languages for her book *Choctalking on Other Realities.* Her books include *Shell Shaker,* 2001; *Evidence of Red,* 2005; *Miko Kings: An Indian Baseball Story,* 2007; and *Choctalking on Other Realities,* which was released in 2013. Kirstin Squint is a professor at High Point University, where she teaches courses in Native American literature and southern literatures. She is the leading scholar on LeAnne Howe's work, and she's currently completing a book on the topic. Again, it was a privilege to sit down and talk to both of them during the Faulkner and Yoknapatawpha Conference, and we're excited to bring you this conversation today.

■ ■ ■

Gina Caison: I am so excited to be here with you guys in Oxford, Mississippi! We are at the Faulkner and Yoknapatawpha Conference, which this year is focusing on Faulkner and Yoknapatawpha and the Native South, which is probably going to inform our conversation in some ways; but I think what we want to do today is focus on this "Native" in the Native South and talk through some issues that some listeners may find familiar and, for others, this may be the first time they've thought about Choctaw people in the South. So, we welcome all. Wherever you are, you can start here. All right, to both of you: why is it important that people currently in the South, for the most part non-Natives, learn and know Native history, Native Nations, and Native cultures from this area?

LeAnne Howe: You know, it's important that people in the South realize that they are living on Native land and the importance of that Native history and how it informs their lives today. By ignoring it, or never having thought of Indians before, you really, if you're a mainstream person, you've really cut yourself out of hundreds and hundreds of years of the experiences of people that came before. I think it's actually harmful to your health in ways that maybe people haven't thought about. For instance, the landscape, the soils, the relationship between flooding and drought, and those kinds of issues are something that Natives dealt with long before Europeans arrived. But if you know nothing about that, you're vulnerable in ways that you may not even realize. So that's why I think it's important to study Native literatures.

Kirstin Squint: You know, one of the things that I think about is really informed by my work on LeAnne's work and thinking about things that she's said. The story of colonialism has always been "How did the Europeans affect the Indigenous people?" But what I think Indigenous Studies is doing for us today is asking us, "Well, how did the Indigenous people affect the Europeans?" If you think about Jace Weaver's *The Red Atlantic* and the question "Would the potato famine have happened had the Indigenous people not introduced the potatoes to Europeans?" Right, those kinds of things are interesting to think about. LeAnne has really, I think, forced me—and I get really excited about this—to think about "What is it about southern culture that is Indigenous?" As Americans, what have we learned from Indigenous people, and how did it change those of us who were descended from colonists? And, of course, what does that mean for everybody living in the South or in the United States today? And then the other thing, and I don't want to start with Removal because that's often the story of the South, but I do want to comment on Removal because I've been teaching a class that deals with Removal. I think that going to that story and then going back from that story is really helpful because people think that they know something about Removal when, in fact, they know very little about it, and then they realize how much more there is and they want to know more. At least that's been the experience I've had with my students.

GC: And to that end, LeAnne, you've written a lot of creative and critical work. How do you see those two informing each other? How do you see your novels and your creative work and your poetry foregrounding this history, these political concerns, and these very real material concerns? What does your creative work bring?

LH: Story. My work is both creatively and critically informed by story. What does that mean? And how to think about story? For instance, the work that I am doing now is informed by stories of Native Christians that go out as missionaries. What was their life about? And in the Southeast, this is something that is well known and well talked about, but you don't see it in contemporary fiction. So that's a story, and I follow it with research. If I wasn't able to do any research on these questions, I think that would negatively impact the story that I want to tell. So—I start with the story, I do a lot of research for my critical work, and then it's plowed into the creative work that I need and want to do.

GC: This historical moment, the thing that catches your eye, and you say, "There's a story there."

LH: Right.

GC: And where does it go?

LH: Where I can take it.

GC: [*to Kirstin*] I know you've taught LeAnne's work a lot; you've read everything. How does it help you when you read the creative work? What does it do for you? How do you use it to teach and to talk to students? Some of your students are Eastern Band, and they may be familiar with these histories. Some students have never thought about this. You said students think they know about Removal; it turns out they know very little. How does a novel like *Shell Shaker* help them get at the truth of historical events through the creative work?

KS: Well, you know, I'm a literature professor, but I'm also coming from a cultural studies background and approach, so *Shell Shaker*, for example, I teach in a class about Removal, and it's a shift for us because we're in North Carolina. I'm teaching a lot of Cherokee works, and we're thinking about Cherokee Removal because that's where we are, and that's what we need to grapple with, but *Shell Shaker* opens up the door to ask, "Hey, what about these other tribes?" Again, very often the conversation is "Oh, I didn't know they were removed," and suddenly the students' research expands as the learning expands. I got a ton of research presentations on Seminoles because they just had no idea. They're like, "Hey, this Osceola guy, wow." It's fantastic that they're finding out and realizing there are so many of those stories they had no idea about. They thought that there was this one thing, so *Shell Shaker* works in this way. *Miko Kings* works very well to talk about the Allotment Act and to talk about the relationships between African Americans and Native Americans.

LH: I mean, at this conference we heard a lot of people talking about the vehicle for change and vehicle for changes. I think that is the essence of what Native literature does. It opens up people to our history and that we are alive and well in the twenty-first century—well, not completely well, but at least alive. Over the decades that I've been teaching, I can't tell you how many times people have said, "Oh, I thought you were all dead." And so that hasn't changed all that much.¹ To go back to your original question, the South would not be the South without Native cultures informing southerners. How did they do that? By hosting immigrants, Natives offered refuge, fed people, for, you know, a hundred years, well, more like seventy or eighty years. We certainly fed the foreigners who were here beginning in the 1690s, 1699. Really, we fed, helped, protected them, and this is a large part of southern culture: to feed is to offer refuge. I mean, the South is known for this, but it's also Native culture that really, really gave this landscape its moral compass. That's not to take anything away from the people who have come; that's just the way that the culture works. And now what's beautiful about this is our culture continues to work. When I look around at the South, I think that the culture is a reflection of us as Native people, as Choctaw, Chickasaw, and as all the other southeastern tribes. The culture itself reflects something that we gave, and now, I think white people are learning more readily about southeastern Indians. Southerners are also giving of themselves. It's a southern lifeway, so to speak, and those things are beautiful and reflective of who we all are.

GC: And I think that's the South at its best.

LH: Yes, at its best.

GC: It's not always at its best.

LH: No, I know! [*Laughing*]

GC: But when we are our best selves, yeah, we are doing things that were learned from what Native people had been doing in this place for thousands of years.

LH: And really the land taught Native people how to be, and so yes, the same can be said for Indians. We aren't always at our best, you know. We are not always our highest selves. It's human nature, but because we were here for a long time, I think it's very important for us to follow our ancestors' examples.

[Music Interlude]

GC: In *Choctalking on Other Realities*, LeAnne, you talk about this concept of "tribalography" and I think it's just a brilliant concept. I know, Kirstin, you've talked a lot about LeAnne's use of this term. I just want to talk about what is tribalography, how do we understand it, and what does it do? How has it been useful in your work, in your life, in your critical work? What does tribalography allow us to see and think about that otherwise hasn't been seen or thought about?

KS: Well, LeAnne talks about this in an essay that came out in about 2001, I think it was, "The Story of America."

LH: It's been a long time now.

KS: Yeah! It's a fascinating essay because she goes into the whole history of the Haudenosaunee Confederacy and the way that they influenced the Founders of the United States, and she talks about story and the way that Natives tell stories. And she talks about this bringing together the "past, present, and future milieu"—I'm actually quoting you there—and Natives and non-Natives in connection to the land. The cool thing that has happened over the last, gosh, I don't know, maybe ten years, is that a lot of scholars, Native Studies scholars, have started trying to figure out how you use tribalography as methodology. For a long time, I referred to it as an aesthetic because I thought, "Oh, this is about the way that Natives tell stories." But there's a way you can apply this, and that's what folks have been doing in Native critical studies.

LH: I thought about this for a long time. I was trying to identify, for non-Indians and non-Indian scholars, what is it about Native literature that makes us both transnational and helps us as we have tried to help newcomers that have come to this land. What is the ingredient that made that possible? And, again, it comes back to story, but the fact that Natives always, always, always are always adding to their story. The method is the addition that you're making—meaning that by adding white people, Black people, other red people, yellow, brown, we are constantly adding to our story. We have met new people from around the world, and that makes us constantly a people who are adaptable, adapting, and open. Additions make equations, and so tribalography tries to make equations of the additions that are coming and all of the changes that are happening in story. If you read a Native novel, you will always have people from all different countries, all different religions included in the story. We don't exclude or cut people off. Now juxtapose that with a non-Native, contemporary novel. We Natives are nowhere in that story. We actually don't exist; hence, people think we're dead. Take anybody's work, an author that you love, we're still, as Native people, nowhere in that story. We don't exist, we're invisible.

KS: I'm thinking about this class that I taught this last fall. It was called American Indian Women Writers. I think there's a temptation sometimes when non-Native scholars who have no familiarity with Native Studies would look at something like *Shell Shaker*, and I'm also thinking about Deborah Miranda's *Bad Indians* because I taught it alongside *Miko Kings*. The thing that I think that some folks might say is "Oh, that's postmodern pastiche" because you're pulling all these things in there. The problem with that is this complete lack of understanding, acknowledgment, or desire to know, or understand, anything about these five hundred-plus Native cultures and the way stories have been traditionally told or that there is a literary tradition among Native peoples.

LH: Native stories have these qualities that you don't find in mainstream literature. I began to think about what we do naturally, as just storytellers and people, and why other kinds of literatures exclude Natives from the story. In fact, they exclude Native history from the story of America. That's really the impetus for writing the essay "The Story of America: A Tribalography." It's also "one thing leads to another," and that's how I work. Right now, I'm interested in how our people looked at the weather patterns.

GC: Well, and I think, too, that it's something in the hard sciences or mathematics that the best equation should be able to account for the most variables, right?

LH: Right.

GC: And, if you have a theory or an equation, and it can't account for the addition of something, and it can't answer that, then you have two options: pretend that other data don't exist, because you want to save your equation, or say, "Maybe this isn't the right equation, and we need to figure out something that can account."

[Music Interlude]

GC: We've been talking a lot the last few days about "the Native South." It seems complicated, hard to define. It encompasses a lot of things, but I know, LeAnne, you had mentioned in some correspondence that we've had before that, as opposed to the Global South and as opposed to all of these other connectivities, how do you think scholars right now are thinking of the Native South? Where can it take us, as a term that can encompass so many people but also not lose tribal specificity, which is incredibly important for nationalism and citizenship?

LH: I think the Native South is an academic fiction in and of itself. I think that because maybe it lacks a southeastern component. Well, yeah, the South is many things, but the southeastern South, our original homelands, are places in which Native people believe we still have purview over the land, and our mother still calls us to return. I'm not sure, in the academic sense, how folks are defining Native South, and then what does that mean when people say the Global South. I, frankly, am confused by that. I also think, are we looking at colonialism worldwide? Is that what you really mean when you say, "the Global South": how Natives were colonized, removed, taken from our mother, our homeland, and placed somewhere else? Is that what you mean by the Global South? That colonizers can do that all over the world? I'm not sure that I'm the right person to answer that because I don't have an answer for how complex the meaning is. The Native South and Southeast, in particular, I know a little bit more about. I know that story, but I'm not sure that's what is meant.

KS: I find it's something I'm really concerned about, how we're defining it and what we're doing with the definition. In the book that I've been working on about LeAnne, one of the things that I do at the beginning is try to look at how people have defined it, so I don't know that I like the term. It's institutionalized though; there's a journal, an interdisciplinary journal, *Native South*, and they defined it as, and I'm going to paraphrase because I don't remember exactly but basically, the people whose ancestral homelands are the South, wherever they may be at this point. So you can talk about Native South, and you can talk about someone like Thomas King in Canada, who's Cherokee. There's that, but other scholars have tried to limit the definition and say, "No, the Native South is only those Indigenous people still remaining in the South." I personally find that definition to be really problematic. I get this from LeAnne and of course you can read about it in lots of things, but in an interview that we did in *MELUS*, she talks about Choctaws picking up handfuls of Mississippi dirt and carrying it with them to Oklahoma. They literally took the land with them. So, okay, what does that mean? The South got transplanted. But the problem I have with the term is that the South usually refers to what we think of as the Confederacy, so that is a colonial construct, right? "Southeastern" seems more appropriate if we're going to talk about it geographically.

LH: I think the Chickasaws are a great model for this idea of the Native South, and certainly my colleague Jodi Byrd would be very keen to remind folks that the Chickasaws have decided to buy back their homelands, one acre at a time, and they're doing it. They're also building a museum; they're very much involved in that idea of returning to Mississippi. They were in the northern part of the state, and the Choctaws were in the south, and then you have a lot of other tribes that were small, living in our proximity like the Houmas, the Chitimachas. All of these things are important, but they're mostly undefined, I think, in this term of the "Native South" because the history is so complicated. The history is so dark with this, "Oh you can't be part of the South; you don't live there anymore." Well, whose fault is that? So you don't get to make those distinctions if you're trying to be inclusive, which I think some people are trying to be exclusive again. They're trying to exclude and pretend that you can keep us out. And isn't that just too bad?

KS: Yeah.

GC: It cuts off your own world.

LH: Right.

[Music Interlude]

KS: I also think, and this is separate but related, I really think that if you know that your family, and of course people who know that they have a family history of slavery, some people have just made reparations because they feel they need to. This is something for me, teaching this class on Removal, particularly in North Carolina. I know some degree of my family history, and I have an ancestor who fought in the American Revolution who basically migrated the family to Kentucky after one of the treaties with the Cherokee, and it couldn't have happened until then. What I think is crazy is that I grew up in Kentucky, and I mean, you grew up in North Carolina, so you had a real awareness of Native people. There's a federally recognized tribe, there are numerous state-recognized tribes. Kentucky has no federally recognized tribes, yet that land would not be that land had it not been for several treaties with the Cherokees, and of course it's a historical hunting ground for the Shawnee. There are all of these salt licks and the Buffalo Trace, and it's a place so rich with Native history but the conversation is—

LH: Absent.

KS: It's absolutely absent except for everybody's got a Cherokee relative.

LH: [*Laughs*]

GC: [*Laughing*] Well, that gets to something else we should talk about, actually, which is why tribal specificity and citizenship are important.

LH: Right.

KS: Well, and as you were talking about this idea that because of casinos, tribes suddenly have a lot of money, so now there are so many more applications for enrollment because people think that they can get ahold of some of that money, which, as you pointed out, is not—

LH: It's silly. They're not really even asking for enrollment; they're just asking for a handout. "Can you give me some money? Give me some money, give me some money, give me some money." Okay.

GC: Well, and also I know that there was an article that just came out about this, something that I think a lot of us in Native Studies have said before, that Cherokee princesses are also about white people attempting to Indigenize their whiteness to the Southeast. It alleviates guilt. It shortcuts any investment in the land, that it's somehow just now transcendent because it's in your fictional "blood." However, there is also a distinction, I think— and being from North Carolina and particularly in eastern North Carolina, I see this distinction—with communities, particularly labeled as "Black communities" in the South that may have *been* Native communities, and keeping in mind that the terms "Black" and "Native" are not mutually exclusive. Some white bureaucrat comes in and decides that the people are either "white or non-white," and in the South, the "non-white" becomes labeled as "Black" by default even if the community is largely made up of Indigenous people. I think there are also complications when you look at Black identity and Native identity in the South, and I'm thinking of the Eastern seaboard, North Carolina tribal peoples specifically. There are a lot of stories about someone else just coming in and making a determination of these people as "non-white, therefore they are Black, and then therefore they are African American." It's another way to simplify and erase and ignore people's stories about themselves. That is not the same as the specious claims to Cherokee princess grandmothers, you know? When I'm talking to people about this, I always try to explain, "We really have two separate issues going on here, always in the service of landed white supremacy."

KS: Indian Removal simplified things in the South for the production of cotton and all sorts of things. It was never that simple of a story, but there were so many state and federally sanctioned people in positions of power, you know, bureaucrats who were moving to make this happen.

LH: Right, so there's that layer, then there's the plain old "My grandmother was a Cherokee Indian princess." That's a story, and I get that story a lot. People just come up and say, "Oh, I'm Indian too." Okay, you know, whatever.

GC: It's also dangerous, too. I think, LeAnne, you've talked about this. It has material implications when people apply for things like scholarships. I think one of your examples, and maybe I'll ask you to talk about this, is how say someone is applying for a scholarship that's supposed to go to someone of a certain citizenry and then they just claim this other thing. In any other context, we would recognize this claim as absurd.

KS: It's so problematic because typically, in these situations, people are asked to self-identify and then are taken at their word. People will choose to identify as Native American without tribal enrollment or proof of it. I could be totally wrong about this, but I don't think people who are more than likely white, and that's obviously a fraught term as well, check "African American," but checking "Native American" will get them something, as we've talked about. The thing is people get jobs. This is a huge controversy in American Indian Studies: people get jobs because they claim to be Native American.

LH: That's right. It just makes me crazy!

KS: Right, and no one has asked them for verification because they are taking them at their word, so the implications become huge. There are real material implications of this, and then Native people who are enrolled are hurt by those sorts of situations.

LH: So the job goes to someone who's passing as Native, who is not enrolled, and they are taken at their word because—why?

KS: I'm very glad that Gina is giving us a very public forum to have this discussion because I do feel that these are the types of conversations that happen at Native Studies conferences or conferences where people are really talking about these kinds of issues. But in a public program we hardly ever have these conversations unless, you know, a new Lone Ranger movie comes out and pretty soon everyone is interviewing you and asking you about Tonto, right? You know what I'm saying? That's the occasion when it happens, often.

LH: Or another writer makes a mistake about thinking they're writing about one thing, and they really don't know what the hell they're writing about. I know J. K. Rowling had used a story, and she talked about the myths of Native people, and it was kind of just an absurd moment, and I thought, "Oh, no. Stick to what you know."

GC: No, I know.

LH: It's like, oh my gosh. Somebody interviewed me from *National Geographic* about her, and I was like, "Well, it's just typical, right?" You know?

GC: Also, make her answer for her, you know?

LH: Right, don't come to me!

GC: Why do Natives, and we do this to a lot of ethnic minorities in this country, but why do you have to answer for J. K. Rowling's mistakes? It's not your responsibility! You are writing your own work! Right, it's like, "If you have any questions about that, I'd be happy to take them." . . . Native people are vocal, they will tell you what they think, and they talk back. And then people like J. K. Rowling will shut down and talk to fans on Twitter about all sorts of things. She's blocking Native Studies scholars who are asking her to account for herself. I wouldn't so much have a problem with it if she was Donald Trump.

LH: But she's not.

[*Laughter*]

GC: She's not, and she tends to parade herself as particularly progressive and liberal.

LH: About everything but Natives.

GC: Well, she just won't have the conversation, and I think, "How progressive are you?" You know what? Just say, "I was wrong."

KS: Right. "I didn't know. I made a mistake."

GC: "I'm willing to learn."

LH: Right, "The End," and everybody shuts up.

[Music Interlude]

GC: What do each of you want to see as the future for Native people of, from the South?

LH: I can say what I would like to happen is for, as part of the Native Southeast or Native South, I'd like to see a lot more conferences that are not just centered around Faulkner because he writes very little about Natives really. There are stereotypes in his fiction, but I would like to see more conferences around Natives and non-Native issues in the South, both historical and contemporary issues. Certainly, the people who stayed behind, the reservation systems, how the South is shaped. I mean, I would really like to see that kind of discussion continue in the future.

KS: I think these conversations are important. I think right now we are at a point where we are not even really sure how to get going or say, "What is the Native South?" I mean, we're still having really seminal conversations. What I want to see happen from those conversations is more teaching in the classroom. I've been talking to different people who are at universities in the South, like Deborah Miranda, Drew Lopenzina, all the folks in Georgia, you all, and Channette Romero, Jace Weaver, people teaching Native lit and Native studies, and I'm really curious about those experiences because I think a lot of folks, particularly folks who teach southern literature, aren't comfortable teaching Native literature. I'd like to see Native literature get into more southern literature classes, but just broadly, more people teaching Native literature in the South.

LH: The conversations that will continue into the twenty-first century, I think, are around these issues and the stories of immigration. "Oh, immigrants are bad." If the public, and scholars were to look at historical America, they'd realize the humor in the fallacy and the tragedy of thinking that immigration is a problem now. And so, that's a way in which Native literature, Native stories, Native histories help white Americans be better prepared in the twenty-first century. We can teach how to talk about even immigration. These kinds of conversations are very important. My vision of the future is that we will have these kinds of conversations, academically and intellectually, with the citizenry of the "Native South."

[Music Interlude]

GC: We'd like to thank LeAnne Howe and Kirstin Squint for sitting down this week for this excellent discussion. Likewise, we'd like to thank Jay Watson and everyone at the University of Mississippi for a very productive Faulkner and Yoknapatawpha Conference on Faulkner and the Native South. Please visit our website aboutsouthpodcast.com to learn more about LeAnne Howe's work as well as find links to where you can acquire your own copy of *Shell Shaker, Miko Kings, Choctalking on Other Realities*, or *Seeing Red. About South* is brought to you each week from the historic West End of Atlanta, Georgia. Kelly Vines is coproducer. Music is by Brian Horton. Please visit his website at brianhorton.com, and please subscribe to *About South* on your preferred podcast platform. Next week, we are talking to Michael Bibler about the B-52s, so brush up on your "Love Shack," and we'll see you next week.

Note

1. Ellipses in this interview indicate text omitted for this volume.—Ed.

Choctaw Tales:
An Interview with LeAnne Howe

Padraig Kirwan / 2016

From *Women: A Cultural Review* 27, no. 3 (2016): 265–79. Reprinted by permission of Taylor and Francis, Ltd.

LeAnne Howe, a citizen of the Choctaw Nation of Oklahoma, is the Eidson Distinguished Professor in American Literature in the Franklin College of Arts and Sciences at the University of Georgia. She has written poetry, fiction, screenplays, plays, creative nonfiction, and critical essays. Her writing is primarily concerned with the experience and the perspectives of American Indian people and communities.[1] These themes—and many others—are explored in her novels, *Shell Shaker* (2001) and *Miko Kings: An Indian Baseball Story* (2007), and the collection of poetry that she published in 2005, *Evidence of Red*. She has received many awards and commendations, all of which are testament to the groundbreaking nature of her work: *Shell Shaker* was the recipient of a Before Columbus Foundation American Book Award (2002); the French translation of the novel, *Equinoxes Rouges*, was a finalist for the 2004 Prix Médicis Étranger; and *Evidence of Red* was the winner of the Oklahoma Book Award for poetry in 2006. More recently, *Choctalking on Other Realities* (2013), a book that Howe describes as "three parts memoir, one part tragedy, one part absurdist fiction, and one part 'marvellous realism,'" won the inaugural Modern Language Association (MLA) Prize for Studies in Native American Literatures, Cultures, and Languages in 2014. The MLA selection committee wrote: "In *Choctalking on Other Realities*, LeAnne Howe integrates high theory with travel narrative, personal reflection, humor, and analysis to craft a formally innovative work of anticolonial literary and cultural criticism that teaches its audiences about the inner workings of Indigenous epistemologies." Along with being the recipient of a United States Artists Ford Fellowship and a Lifetime Achievement Award from the Native Writers Circle of the Americas, Howe also received the 2015 Western Literature Association Distinguished Achievement Award, a prize that "honors transformative contributions to the field of Western American literary studies."

Her interviewer, Padraig Kirwan, is a Senior Lecturer in the Department of English and Comparative Literature at Goldsmiths, University of London. He has published essays in *Novel: A Forum on Fiction, Comparative Literature,* and the *Journal of American Studies.* His book *Sovereign Stories: Aesthetics, Autonomy, and Contemporary Native American Writing* (2013) examines the fiction and poetry of several Native American authors, including LeAnne Howe.

Howe's work might be described as enlivening, eclectic, and often hectic, and, more often than not, she brings together a plethora of stories concerning the historical and contemporary experiences of the Choctaw Nation. Various geographical, spiritual, familial, and narratological spaces are revealed or plotted during the course of Howe's narratives, and, as a consequence, images that relate to the act of mapping, the basis of storytelling, and the subject of community and place become recurring motifs throughout her writing. Concerned with the ways in which Choctaw lifeways have been mapped out across time, Howe appears to be especially interested in the representation of travel, exchange, contact, and consumption not only in the precontact and postcontact United States, but also within the global village. Rather than compartmentalizing past and present-day experiences into discrete, autonomous spaces, her critical essays and fictional storylines establish a kaleidoscopic perspective that provides the reader with a powerful sense of the connectedness that informs and shapes events in the Choctaw world and beyond. Accordingly, Howe focuses on moments of exchange and trade between the tribes and, latterly, between the tribes and the colonizers, and her writing pays considerable attention to transactions that occur in a number of key locations: narrative sites, bodily sites, spiritual sites, national and international sites, and so on. As such, her books, poems, and essays examine and reflect on the tribe's relationship to place, to the spirit world, to cosmological forces, to the American continent, and to the world. A crucial aspect of this exploration of Choctaw presence is the interrogation of movement within, and between, key sites inhabited by Indigenous peoples, and her work often deals with the questions of sovereignty, continuance, and self-determination across a number of contested, and often overlapping, spaces.

Howe's coinage of the term "tribalography," and her continued engagement with a creative vision of communal values, has helped her readers to better understand, and focus on, the web of being that orders the Choctaw world. By engaging with Howe's multilayered, multipointed canvases, a new generation of Native Studies scholars has delved into many of the complexities of the Choctaw worldview, underlined continued Indigenous presence, examined the meeting point between Indigenous peoples and colonial "pathfinders," differentiated between confirmatory and detrimental forms of exchange and communication (in both precontact and postcontact times), and, above all, considered the ways in which Indigenous writers shape the world through their fiction. Howe's writing demonstrates how, exactly, a web of contiguous, interrelated stories might map out moments of cross-cultural contact, colonial movement, consumption, and (inter)national trade. In doing so, she underlines the extent to which colonization is reliant on not only particular forms of commerce and exploitation, but also trade, tyranny, and movement within a given territory.

Padraig Kirwan: What have been the main incentives and motivations for you as a writer? Have you found yourself returning to the same well, so to speak?

LeAnne Howe: Let me begin by saying I'm really grateful to you for asking these questions. I'm really honored that you've seriously engaged with my work. I can't think of anything better! I mean that sincerely, from my heart.

PK: It's always a pleasure!

LH: Let me start, then, by saying that my reasons for writing *Shell Shaker*, which really kicked off my career nearly seventeen years ago, was that it occurred to me as I was travelling around with short stories and things of this nature, and poetry, that no one seemed to know anything about Choctaw people. Nothing. They had never heard of the tribe.

PK: Wow!

LH: This is the United States of course. No one knew where our tribe came from; they had never heard of Choctaws; they couldn't think of a Choctaw work that was integrated into the English language. Nothing. I began to think about that, why that was, and what could I do to help to introduce Choctaws, in the past and present, to a broader, mainstream audience. So I began working on *Shell Shaker*, and it was ten years before I got it to a publisher. It was ten years in the making. I went to the Smithsonian Institution on a Native American internship; at the time, I wanted to look at Cyrus Byington's notes on changes in the Choctaw language. Later, I went to the Newberry Library in Chicago as part of Indian Voices in the Academy, investigating the Karpinski Map Collection. I worked in Jackson, Mississippi, archives, where I met Pat Galloway, who was really an expert in eighteenth-century Choctaw history . . . an expert in French writings in the eighteenth century, so I was lucky. Galloway said, "You have to go there and look at the maps, look at where people were." That really began that process of pushing me to become a better writer and a better historian of my own people.

PK: I see.

LH: And that was significant. Writing itself, the craft of writing? I used to think I was a minimalist. [*Laughs*]

PK: [*Laughs*] Really?

LH: Yeah, I'm a minimalist. No, I'm *nothing like* a minimalist [*laughter*]. Basically, I told this story [*Shell Shaker*], and it had to be told out of time because I had to start with the twentieth century and move in and out of that to be able to interest people about how we are in the present and in the past—how we're shaped by our past. All of that is to say that that was my impetus for writing *Shell Shaker*. I have continued to go back to Choctaw people with *Miko Kings: An Indian Baseball Story*, in which I look at the way that Indians play baseball. Then, looking at it, I thought, "You know, we *invented* the American pastime."

PK: Yes!

LH: That has raised a lot of eyebrows, but then you can look at our lifeways mapped onto baseball: playing the game counterclockwise; having the ball man in the center of the game; a game without time; a game that runs in four directions; a game that takes people home, which is the returning home, the art of return—which happens at all these mound complexes. That really interested me. So I wrote a book about baseball. [*Aside*] Something I didn't know anything about, to tell the truth! Since then, I have continued to work on telling Choctaw stories, certainly. In my scholarship, tribalography comes out of looking at the ways Native people, certainly Choctaw people, tell stories. One thing leads to another; we don't leave out the French in our stories, we don't leave out the Irish in our stories, and we don't leave out mainstream, white people, in our stories either. Or Black people, or Asian people. We're supposed to tell stories that include *everybody*. Hence this idea about unity in my work. I'm still returning to that well. Although I've just finished a manuscript called *Savage Conversations* about Mary Todd Lincoln and the savage that she invented—an American Indian that she said nightly tortured her. The novel that I'm working on now is set in the Middle

East, in Bilad Al-Sham in 1913—with a Choctaw man going as a Christian missionary—and I've not gone to that well. He gets caught up in the Arab Revolt of 1916 and fights alongside the Arabs. Then his relatives come looking for him nearly a century later, or, rather, looking for his legacy there. I find that my own tribal stories are really the base, the core narrative, from which I try to reach out to other parts of the world.

PK: There's so much in that answer! And it's fantastic to listen to you talk about those influences. To go back to your opening point, it always surprises me, as someone who works in the field of Native American literature, that so many Americans are unfamiliar with the literature and are unfamiliar with the tribes. Unfamiliarity with tribal lifeways and art might be expected further afield, but to hear you say that your initial experience was that American people knew very little about the Choctaw, or about tribal lifeways, and didn't understand how integrated tribes are to the whole in the US is always shocking.

LH: It *is* shocking, isn't it?

PK: It really is.

LH: That brings me to the other side of that story, which relates to acts of giving. That's embedded in *Shell Shaker* in the fact that the Choctaws heard about the potato famine—the Irish potato famine—in 1847; they heard about it. In Skullyville, they give money [to the Irish]; they give what they can, and donate this money for the Irish famine relief, for the Irish people. People they have never seen or heard of. Maybe they had met people who said, "Well, I'm from Ireland," or who had Irish ancestors, but they, the Choctaws, hadn't been to Ireland in 1847! But that relationship of giving is something that I write about in *Shell Shaker*, and it becomes part of a bigger narrative and the reason that James Joyce becomes a character—I'm trying to pay homage to Irish storytelling and the relationships that we have with Irish people. As a result, you and I are doing a book on transatlantic exchange—*Transatlantic Reciprocity: The Choctaw and the Irish*—between the Irish and the Choctaw. And this gift that keeps on recurring between our two nations is significant and very powerful and very personal to Choctaw people.

PK: Indeed.

LH: I just gave a talk in Durant, in our tribal complex, earlier on this month about that 1847 gift. All of the Choctaw women in the audience—there were 275—they all knew about it. They all had talked about it. They all knew what that gift meant: *ima*, to give without strings. And I was *so* proud of the community at that point, thinking, "Yes, we know. We're supposed to give." And that's the role of women. It tickles me that you and I are able to create this book and to think a little more deeply about what these gifts are signifiers of.

PK: Definitely. Following on from that and following on from this idea of international connections, you do seem to travel quite a bit, as so many internationally well-known authors are compelled to do. Do you find that your time as a Fulbright Scholar in Jordan, as well as your time spent giving lectures and readings abroad, informs your work?

LH: Absolutely. Absolutely. Working with people who are different from you is "Tribalism 101." This is what our people and the installation of the mantel that a person carries as a traveler [do]: be the creative expression of your tribe, but also learn and return that knowledge to your community as the *fani mikos* of old would do. To learn about what the other person's point of view is, then return home and tell your own community about how other people live and feel about their lives—that's tribalism. And it's something I think that comes from our deep, deep cultural ecology in the Southeast. I think of myself—[*aside*] if it's not too much a case of bragging—I think of myself in this old-fashioned way: my job as a writer is to learn from other people and to express that back to my own community, or the country that I live in, or even to the stories that I tell, and that kind of exchange makes me a better writer.

PK: That's so interesting because that's very much part of what we are doing in our own project, but there is, of course, a long history of those types of exchanges, and it's fascinating to me that your work ties in with that. Of course, it ties in with many themes and forms!

LH: [*Laughs*] Thank you.

PK: You tend to work with a plethora of literary forms and scholarly or storytelling mediums. As well as publishing award-winning collections such as *Evidence of Red: Poems and Prose* and fiction such as *Shell Shaker*, you have written critical essays, performed in one-woman adaptations of your own work, and been the screenwriter for documentaries such as *Indian Country Diaries: Spiral of Fire*. How important is variation to your process as a writer and an artist?

LH: Well, it's kind of the case that one thing leads to another. This is my idea of tribalography, of adding to your own sense of your work. For me, writing a play about a particular subject just seems [*pauses*] it's a different way to tell a story, but it's also a way to engage a very different kind of audience. In fact, *Sideshow Freaks and Circus Injuns* just received funding for a production in August 2017 in Toronto. That play has its roots in my Aunt

Euda's performing Indian in the circus. We found that synergy and noted that when the exhibitors put on the World's Fair in St. Louis in 1904, they destroyed sixteen mounds to put up a Ferris wheel![2]

PK: They really did that at the time? I never knew that! The disrespectfulness and the lack of cultural understanding still shock me to the core.

LH: Oh, yeah. And that's even beside the fact that Monique [Mojica, Guna and Rappahannock, playwright and performer] and I had relatives who went into the circus as performers. But the other piece of that story, land-wise, is that mound sites around the United States became hosts to the nineteenth- and twentieth-century circuses.

PK: That's an amazing historical detail. It's so disturbing too. Is Monique working closely with you on that project?

LH: Yes, we are cocreators of the play *Sideshow Freaks and Circus Injuns.*

PK: We'll be watching out for that! Speaking of collaboration, did you realize how important the term "tribalography" would become when you first coined it, or envisage a time when the concept would be the focus of a special edition of a journal such as *Studies in American Indian Literature*? Is it now hard to fathom why the embodiment of tribal understandings had been overlooked for so long?

LH: Well, I'll answer the first part. No, I *didn't*!

PK: [*Laughs*]

LH: I thought I was kind of clever, but not so clever! Nancy Shoemaker, at the time, had invited me to write an essay for her book *Clearing a Path*, which is about ways of thinking about Indian history and, for me, Indian story. So I looked at all my contemporaries, right? I looked at the way in which they were telling stories in their novels or poetry, and always they were adding to other stories. There were openings, and they were adding. Almost all Native literature engages the white man, the Black man, the Black man and woman. They were engaging the world around them. I asked myself, "Why is it that Natives are nowhere in white mainstream literature? Nowhere!" We don't exist for those authors. I was trying to take that high road and say, "Look, we're perfectly competent in telling stories that engage you. But you leave us out of the stories. And we're left out of America's stories." That was the whole impetus for tribalography. I was surprised that people took it as seriously; it took a long time for it to catch on—it came out in 2001, something like that. I've been very pleased that scholars, young scholars and old scholars—[*aside*] well, not so many old scholars, but younger scholars!—have said, "Well, this is a way to think about Native stories." So, that's been really delightful—that I've been helpful to people trying to understand the way that Native people tell stories and *what we want*. We want, I think, reciprocity. We want that reciprocity.

PK: That comes through so clearly in your work and projects.

LH: Again, I'm going to mention our book, *Transatlantic Reciprocity*! This is something that you and I are engaged in: trying to show reciprocity in action. The Irish have engaged with the Choctaw and continue to have a reciprocal relationship with us. Doesn't that seem right to you?

PK: Yes, it's entirely apposite. And thinking about reciprocity in regards to the term "tribalography," I think that it's useful to think not only about its critical generosity, which is very much in keeping with the manner in which you mobilize connection points in your work. I think that's why your critical work is so easily adaptable and so very useful for scholars. To return to the second part of the question for just a moment: I'm conscious that so many tribal writers were working on questions concerning embodiment, were thinking about tribal lifeways and understandings, but that there wasn't perhaps a specific phrase that pointed towards that reality in a certain way, or a unifying phrase that might have been useful to critics from various tribal backgrounds. Do you think that is why tribalography becomes so manifestly useful in the twenty-first century?

LH: Yes. I mean, I turn to someone like Jill Doerfler, who is a professor at the University of Minnesota, Duluth, who has seriously used tribalography to describe Anishinaabe stories. I thought that works absolutely perfectly, to my mind, to explain how their stories work and worked within the community. I'm gonna back up here a little; in 1987, Roxy Gordon and I wrote *Indian Radio Days*, which was a play.

PK: Okay.

LH: We performed it with our friends; we performed all over Dallas. When I got to the University of Iowa—I was living there and worked at the international education center—we formed "WagonBurner Theatre Troop."

PK: [*Laughs*]

LH: And we went all over the Midwest performing *Indian Radio Days*. But I always said, and Roxy always said—he's passed away—"Take the play and make it your own." So, if the Lakota and Dakota in North and South Dakota want to perform this play, they have to change some of the sight gags to be specific to their own tribes. Well, that's precisely what happened. The Lakota, the Dakota out at Vermillion, South Dakota, picked up the play. It's gone all over the country, with people knowing that the playwrights want them to rewrite sections that could fit their own tribe experiences. That was very influential to me when looking at the idea of a tribalography. For Jill Doerfler to use it just makes sense to me; it just feels right to take these concepts and work with them within their own community, and then make them *your* own. And so that's my sense of the theatrical movement that's happened, the way tribalography has spread, and how baseball is played: "Take this game and make it your own."

PK: I like that notion of performance and how these things work out in various contexts.

LH: Yeah!

PK: Now, in 2015, the folks in the Western Literature Association decided that you should receive the association's Distinguished Achievement Award. What does it mean to you to be placed alongside authors such as Louise Erdrich, Gerald Vizenor, Joy Harjo, William Kittredge, Rudolfo Anaya, and Joan Didion?

LH: I was astounded! Shocked.

PK: It was so well earned and a lovely moment of recognition.

LH: I was so honored to be in the good company of those amazing writers that I couldn't really believe that they meant me! I felt humbled. I really was humbled and grateful to be included in that kind of company. And, you know, these are—if you don't get your head inflated!—moments that are really meaningful to a writer. Then you come home, and you get back to work, and you and I are working on our books and other projects, trying not to be too disgustingly overconfident!

PK: You never are [*laughter*]!

LH: I hope not [*laughter*].

PK: To save you from having to be too deferential, we'll move on. Are there any particular authors whom you would describe as being specifically important influences to your own work?

LH: Well, of course, you know there are so many writers that I love: Sherwin Bitsui, Susan Power, Louise Erdrich. Heid Erdrich's poetry is *amazing*! She just knocks my socks off. But I'm also compelled by Native scholars like P. Jane Hafen, Brenda Child, Jeani O'Brien—especially her book *Firstings and Lastings*—and I read these folks widely. Layli Long Soldier is a new and upcoming Native poet; Natalie Diaz is an amazing poet, and so is Joan Naviyuk Kane, and, of course, my good friend Joy Harjo. . . . All of these writers are important to me. But you know what? I think that one of the writers that I have read and continue to read and be astounded by is the late French writer Marguerite Duras.

PK: I haven't read her work.

LH: Well, she has a minimalist style [*laughs*].

PK: Unlike your own style [*laughter*]!

LH: I write nothing like her. I wish I could. But I just remember thinking her work was poetry, fiction, a screenplay, and so much is said in images. So, I was reading her, reading the work, the fiction, as . . . in fact she says in one of her novels, maybe *Blue Eyes, Black Hair*, that "This is a film." And I thought, "Wow! That really is interesting to me" that she saw the work in cinematic ways. I've been very interested in her and how she came to that. We have many literary ancestors. And I know you do too—have many people who shaped you as a writer. I know that you're compelled by Seamus Heaney. Aren't we all? Aren't we all? Aren't we lucky to have lived in these times, with such amazing ancestors?

PK: Most certainly. It makes a lot of sense to me when you talk not so much about minimalism, perhaps, but rather the image itself, and even that imagist sense of capturing something specific. In *Shell Shaker* and *Miko Kings*, your descriptions are very often focused on framing or seizing one particular image or one particular moment. I've been fortunate enough to hear you talk about your work a few times and to hear you reading. Having done so, I think that the idea of the broad sweep and that sense of the cinematic, which naturally includes the specific—images, moments brought into stark relief—is indeed very much part of your work. That makes perfect sense. Of course, with that, it really is the case that the interweave between Indigenous story, critical theory, and tribal history is vital to any understanding of Choctaw literature, isn't it?

LH: Right! Also, I'm interested in your work and the work of other non-Native scholars such as Chad Allen, Dean Rader, David Stirrup, and the great non-Native women scholars who are working in the field such as Susan Bernardin, Penny Kelsey, Patrice Hollrah, and Lisa Tatonetti. I also read the work of younger scholars in our field—well, they seem young to me: Jodi Byrd, Kirstin Squint, and younger still, the strong PhD candidates that are up and coming, such as Eman Ghanayem and Melissa Slocum. You are all, to me, part of the orbit of my literary world because I read all of you. And I'm grateful for the great work that's going on. So, in some ways, I can't think of a better century to be working in Native studies.

PK: On that note, the past twenty years have seen a real proliferation in terms of the number of scholars working in the field of Native American literary studies. What do you think the next twenty years might hold?

LH: Well, I hope I'm cognizant enough to notice! Undemented, as they say! I also hope that I'm still part of the conversation too! You know, I think that there is a real synthesis going on currently between music, film, and video that is at work in Native culture. And, of course, we can just look at what happened today: Bob Dylan winning the Nobel Prize for Literature! When I think Dylan, I think of one song as being emblematic, and that's the track that says "You're gonna have to serve somebody."

PK: "It may be the Devil / Or it may be the Lord."

LH: [*Laughs*] That's an expression of literature, really. And Native literature is about serving someone; look at what our stories about being in service have done over the last several hundred years. That story of being in service is how you and I connected over the Irish and the Choctaw being in a relationship. The Choctaw held fast to that idea of being in service: "Send money, they're starving." Choctaws sent money to countries all over the world. Sometimes we sent food. When 9/11 happened in New York . . . a giant group of people sent trucks, all kinds of implements, firemen . . . we sent money and people to help. That's being of service. And, in some ways, Bob Dylan winning the Nobel Prize reminds us that literature and literary production—in whatever form it takes—and music, film, poetry, and story is really the next synthesis. Trans-genre is really where it's going. I may not be on the cutting edge of other trends, but that's what I see now.

PK: That's fantastic. Interestingly, some colleagues and I were contacted by various media outlets prior to the announcement of the Nobel Prize committee and asked whether we would like to speak about the work of one of the "likely winners." Ngugi wa Tiong'o, Haruki Murakami, Philip Roth, Joyce Carol Oates, and others were mentioned, but no one mentioned Bob Dylan!

LH: Oh, so they didn't think of him? Regardless, it is so exciting, and today is such a great day! I can't wait to get to my class at the University of Georgia; we're working with sound poems and I've been pushing them to work with sound. And now Bob Dylan wins the Nobel Prize for Literature today. So I'm going in, fully armed [*laughter*]!

PK: Teaching opportunities just fall into your lap sometimes, don't they [*laughter*]? On a slightly separate note, there is a wonderful moment in *Miko Kings* when Ezol Day, the young spirit who has returned to Ada, Oklahoma, says, "Choctaws and Chickasaws are renowned for their ability to rebuild. . . . We seem to manifest nature itself, as re-creators" (34). Occasions of travel—be it across time or space—and instances of recreation are vital to your writing, aren't they?

LH: [*Nods agreement*] And, guess what? The Choctaws are building new mounds in Oklahoma as we speak. As we are talking, they are building three new mounds and a new tribal complex. Now, mound-building hasn't happened in, well, two thousand years. But it's happening now, and the vision and the community at large, in seeing itself as being confident enough to build new mounds, are pretty astounding! When I gave a recent talk to Choctaw women in Durant, Oklahoma, I looked across at the women there, and I said, "Well, I have to say that I am thrilled to be here because fifteen years ago I wrote that the Choctaws were going to build a mound over a terrible leader when I wrote about *Shell Shaker*'s Redford McAlester, and here we are today building three new mounds." And they were, like, "Oh yeah" [*laughs*]. I shouldn't have brought up the bad guy, but I did in a very vague way! [*Jokes*] Oh, I just had to brag to everybody there.

PK: It's a nice segue of sorts, insofar as in this current moment we're dealing, internationally, with a growing sense of isolationism, politically, and the notion of the bad guy is extremely current, given the rise of populism and so on. Your writing focuses not only on Choctaw lifeways, but also points of connection that may help us to think about re-creation and so on. Do you think those perspectives might help us to fight against those who want to pull up the drawbridges, build the wall, or fight whatever version of isolation we're faced with?

LH: I honestly don't know, but I'm going to put my faith, at this moment in time, in the American people. We are *not* isolationists at heart; we are a nation currently being placed under stress by vulgar harbingers of death. In every instance—and this is what makes the Nobel Prize in literature so important—our art speaks to us about being our highest selves, being a lover of humanity. And I believe that the American people will not stand for isolationism, and we're not going to build stupid walls! I just came back from Mexico, and the Mexican people are really so sweet about it, but they're hurt by the way that these characterizations by Donald Trump misrepresent Mexican people. People on the bus who you talk to, they're hurt by this, and they know that they are not these stereotypes. And I *know* that the American people will not, will *not*, build another stupid wall. I know they've started building it, but I don't think it's going anywhere.

PK: That's good news. You reveal a lot in *Choctalking on Other Realities*, be it about your time on Wall Street, early forays in writing, and trips to Japan and elsewhere. Writing is obviously an intensely personal act for you as well.

LH: Yeah, but don't you think it is for all scholars and writers? It's intensely personal because we want to get our ideas across, don't you think?

PK: Yes, yes, I do.

LH: It's very personal, and yet I feel as though—and maybe this is just because I'm so damn old!—that I've got something to say now, something that I might not have been able to say twenty years ago. So, I'm hoping that my new work will be able to sustain itself into the twentieth century. [Hopefully, it will do so because I write about] the Middle East or the ways in which Mary Todd Lincoln—who was very much the Donald Trump of her day—invented a stereotype of an American Indian that tortured her every night. She never met any American Indians that I find in my research, but she invents this savage in her mind, and in her imagination this figure cuts her up, that scalps her, that cuts a bone out of her cheek.[3] . . . So, really, in history we can find these bellicose Trumps. Of course, she was in the asylum, and the doctors there hoped to cure her of her delusions. We haven't gotten there yet with Trump, but perhaps one day!

PK: Well, hopefully! Of course, those invisible presences are so prominent in the nineteenth century and the literature. One thinks of Hawthorne and others. The notion of the haunting is so often there. Speaking of visibility, you've published with Aunt Lute for a long time now. Is there a particular form of solidarity to be found in working with a publishing house that has championed the work of amazing feminist authors and critics such as Gloria Anzaldúa, Paula Gunn Allen, and Audre Lorde? Has that been a very productive relationship for you?

LH: It absolutely has. Aunt Lute is terrific to work with. They're currently bringing out a new anthology by South Asian women writers, *Good Girls Marry Doctors*, edited by Piyali Bhattacharya. I recommend it. As for me, I wanted to put my money where my mouth was, be at a house that valued women, so Aunt Lute was the perfect place, and has been the perfect place, for me to publish. Choctaw women are at the center of their homes and house, so it just seemed like a great place to strike up a relationship. Aunt Lute has been an amazing publishing house to be with for almost twenty years now. I joined up in 2000, so I guess it's almost seventeen years now, and [during that time] Aunt Lute's concerns have been my concerns; having the stories of women, in the center of the universe, is at the heart of their mission. Isn't that cool? And, by the way, they are one of the few feminist presses that have survived.

PK: That's so true. When you think about it, there were a number of presses on the West Coast, in particular, and a number of them have gone to the wall.

LH: They're gone, except Aunt Lute.

PK: Why do you think that is?

LH: I think it is because they've systematically been driven out of business by distributors.

PK: So it's ideologically driven?

LH: It's systematic, and you can guess how and why. There's a movement to try and drive all of these small presses out of business. Kill competition, especially women-centered work. They've done a hell of a job, you know. I'll just say, from my own point of view, if you look at these mega-conglomerates, there's no house, there's no bookstore. . . . You never know what might be available then, and, by closing, or by helping to drive small independent bookstores out of business, you also take the presses with you. I think that's on purpose. I'm not a conspiracy theorist, but if [a large conglomerate owns] the distribution, then how will small presses survive?

PK: I'm glad to say that we have a new independent bookstore called The Word in New Cross beside Goldsmiths. It's the first one that we've had in the neighborhood in some time.

LH: Hooray!

PK: Hopefully, it's a sign of things to come. The millennials are so wary of the big corporations.

LH: The millennials here are starting their own publishing houses, and they are doing great. They *are* the future, and I think that will help. A lot of the millennials driving those initiatives are women, and it was women who organized small presses in the past. So it's happening, but it is slow.

PK: Well, as Hillary Clinton has argued, a revolution takes twenty years of hard work, right?

LH: [*Laughter*] Thank you so much for this chat.

PK: It's been a pleasure, and great fun, as always. Thank you!

Notes

1. Those of us who work in the field of Native American studies and scholars who are Native American/American Indian often move freely between those two terms; this is in recognition of the fact that the terms are widely used in Indian Country by tribal communities. There has been a particular revival of the use of "American Indian" on the grounds that this is the term used in the treaties. [All notes with this interview and all ellipses and bracketed insertions within the interview are from the original publication.—Ed.]

2. Howe's Choctaw ancestors were mound-builders, and her people are noted as being numbered among the ancient mound civilizations that once inhabited southeastern North America. The mounds built by the ancestors continue to be revered sites, and

Nanih Waiya, which is located in Mississippi, is the mound that the Choctaw hold most sacred.

3. Although she is primarily seen as preening, self-regarding, and overly exacting— with very good reason—Mary Todd Lincoln is seen by some as a woman who suffered from disabling poor health, mental infirmity, and the rigors of a bitterly hard life (she lost three sons to early deaths among other tribulations). For instance, around the time of the Abraham Lincoln Presidential Library and Museum special exhibit, "Mary Todd Lincoln: First Lady of Controversy," *Newsweek* ran an article by Karen Springen that included a quotation from Jason Emerson, author of *The Madness of Mary Lincoln*, in which he said that Abraham Lincoln's wife "suffered from bipolar disorder throughout her life." The article also pointed out that several "prominent historians disagree" with Emerson's opinion. One of them, Jean Baker, author *of Mary Todd Lincoln: A Biography*, told *Newsweek* that Mary Todd was "neurotic and narcissistic" but that she would not quite "go with this insanity bit." Troublingly, Mary Todd Lincoln put many of her pains down to the workings of a malevolent American Indian spirit, which she claimed was attacking her.

Works Cited

Howe, LeAnne. *Choctalking on Other Realities*. Aunt Lute Books, 2013.

Howe, LeAnne. *Miko Kings: An Indian Baseball Story*. Aunt Lute Books, 2007.

"LeAnne Howe Wins MLA Prize for *Choctalking on Other Realities*." Aunt Lute Books, 11 Nov. 2016, http://auntlute.com/7093/new_release/leanne-howe-wins-mla-prize -for-choctalking-on-other-realities/.

"MFAW Faculty Member LeAnne Howe to Receive WLA Distinguished Achievement Award." Vermont College of Fine Arts, 11 Nov. 2016, http://vcfa.edu/writing/news /mfaw-faculty-member-leanne-howe-receive-wla-distinguished-achievement-award.

Springen, Karen. "'Hellcat or Helpmate': A Look at Mary Todd Lincoln." *Newsweek*, 19 Sept. 2007, http://europe.newsweek.com/hellcat-or-helpmate-look-mary-todd -lincoln-100149?rm=eu.

Interview with Poet LeAnne Howe

Jeremy Reed / 2017

From University of Tennessee Writers in the Library Blog, February 1, 2017. Reprinted by permission of University of Tennessee Writers in the Library Blog.

It is our great pleasure to be hosting poet, essayist, scholar, and more—LeAnne Howe—for our next Writers in the Library Reading Series Event. You can find out more at our website or on our Facebook or Twitter pages.

Jeremy Reed: We often think of writers as poets, playwrights, novelists, or essayists. We don't often think of a writer as all of those things at once, and yet your writing incorporates multiple genres often. How do you think the process of working in multiple genres has affected your creative life?

LeAnne Howe: You left out scholar. I also produce literary scholarship in my field, Native American literatures. Hubris made me say this, forgive me! But to answer your question, I truly never think about what kind of work belongs in a certain genre. I'm more comfortable letting the work choose how it wants to be experienced in the world. Sounds a bit wacky, but that's how I work. I start out writing what I think will be a poem, and it turns into drama and fiction. That's how *Savage Conversations* was born; it began as poetry, now it's a drama for the stage, and at the same time it's poetry.

My literary ancestry began with the stories my grandmother and great aunts told at family gatherings. Storytelling came first. I was also a journalist for several years, so literary scholarship seemed a reasonable creative move. My career has been a tribalography, my term for the way American Indians tell stories—in multiple genres. And one thing leads to another.

The effect of writing in multiple genres is that I manage to stay busy. At this time, I'm working on a new documentary film, *Searching for Sequoyah*. The website is now up at http://searchingforsequoyah.com/. This summer in Toronto, Canada, we go into rehearsals for a new play I'm coauthoring with Monique Mojica, *Sideshow Freaks and Circus Injuns*. We are performers in the show. Monique is a wonderful actress, teacher, and playwright. We also have many Native collaborators from the southeastern tribes. The show is scheduled to open on August 24, 2017. I'm also finishing a novel this semester. Again, the effect on my creative life is that I am busy, but I don't think this is much different from most artists.

JR: In addition to writing as much as you do, you're the Eidson Distinguished Professor at the University of Georgia. How does teaching relate to your writing life?

LH: I'm very fortunate. Teaching and research are a creative symbiosis for me. My teaching is fueled by my research interests. And vice versa.

JR: You're known as a writer who writes humor exceptionally well. What do you think the role of humor is in writing today?

LH: Humor disarms the reader, disarms an audience. I use it to help readers enter a Native story without feeling guilty about the genocide that was enacted against our ancestors, our tribe, and families. And I've always wanted to be thought of as a female Will Rogers pointing out ironies and absurdities for a bilious public. Hubris made me say this, forgive me!

JR: Your most recent book, *Choctalking on Other Realities*, concerns your experiences traveling the world and representing American and Native identities abroad. In that collection, you write: "Native stories are power." Yet, too frequently, Native writers are left out of conversations about contemporary American literature. What recent Native writers' works do you admire and wish had a wider audience?

LH: I'm very interested in the work of Tommy Pico, a Native poet. I'm reading *IRL*, his first book of poetry. But really, I could name fifty-seven Native writers, and most people will never have heard of them or read their work. Perhaps it is our invisibility in the literary world. Recently I was talking to a group of people about Louise Erdrich's work. They'd never heard of her.

JR: Your newest project, *Savage Conversations*, centers around Mary Todd Lincoln's claims that a "savage Indian" would torture her each night while she was in an insane asylum in 1875. How has writing about this topic affected your concern regarding how Native stories are represented in American history?

LH: We're not represented at all. We get about a paragraph, so to speak, in US students' K–12 education, and we're represented as past tense, dead. All gone. Alas.

Historians and authors interested in the Lincolns knew about the period in Mary Todd Lincoln's life in which she blamed an Indian spirit for her madness. But they ignored it. Why? This is the question I asked when I began researching Mary Todd Lincoln. It felt very much like the 1995 case of Susan Smith from South Carolina, who blamed a Black man for kidnapping her children. People may remember that Smith killed her children then claimed a Black man drove off with them in her car. Both women blamed the "Other" for their insanity. The "why" question is something I try and answer in the book.

Working on *Savage Conversations* has given me insights into how a president's wife in 1875 imagined American Indians. She imagined us as savages. It helped me consider that perhaps Abraham Lincoln thought Dakota Indians were savages. He ordered the execution of thirty-eight Dakota Indians for participation in the so-called Dakota Uprising in 1862 in Minnesota. I don't agree that just because he spared the lives of over two hundred other Dakotas that this is an indication of mercy or that he saw them as human beings. That's not what he says.

Jeremy Michael Reed is a PhD student in creative writing at the University of Tennessee. His poems are published in Public Pool, Still, Valparaiso Poetry Review, *and elsewhere.*

An Interview with LeAnne Howe

Rebecca Macklin / 2017

From *Wasafiri: The Magazine of International Contemporary Writing*, May 19, 2017. Reprinted by permission of Susheila Nasta, Editor-in-Chief.

"A story is active, and a story changes the world. A story is changing the world as I write this."

LeAnne Howe is an enrolled citizen of the Choctaw Nation of Oklahoma, a scholar, and a writer of fiction, poetry, creative nonfiction, and plays. She is the Eidson Distinguished Professor in American Literature in the English Department at the University of Georgia and a former Fulbright Scholar.

Her first novel, *Shell Shaker* (Aunt Lute Books, 2001), received an American Book Award in 2002 from the Before Columbus Foundation. *Evidence of Red* (Salt Publishing, 2005) won the Oklahoma Book Award for poetry in 2006 and the 2006 Wordcraft Circle Award. Her latest two books—*Choctalking on Other Realities* (Aunt Lute Books), a memoir, and *Seeing Red: Hollywood's Pixeled Skins—American Indians and Film* (Michigan State University Press), a coedited anthology of film reviews—were both published in 2013. In August this year, her latest play, *Sideshow Freaks and Circus Injuns*, will premier in Toronto, Canada.

LeAnne met Rebecca Macklin in Mystic Lake, Minnesota, at the Native American Literature Symposium (NALS). This conversation took place over email in the weeks following.

Rebecca Macklin: Thinking about your journey as a writer, I want to ask what led you into your writing path? And which authors have been influential to you?

LeAnne Howe: My grandmother was a storyteller, so I grew up hearing stories, learning natural rhythms that must occur in stories well told. I applied that to my own work when I started writing.

Vine Deloria, in particular, was a great influence on me. He was an intellectual and a writer who was at times polemic, but he asked important questions of non-Indians. By reading Vine's work, *Custer Died for Your Sins*, *American Indian Policy in the Twentieth Century*, *God Is Red*, especially these early works, I learned about my own questions that I wanted to ask in my work. He also gave me courage to perform and write.

RM: As a writer who works in so many forms, how do your scholarship and your creative writing—fiction, poetry, scriptwriting—influence each other and intersect?

LH: My creative interests, these days, drive my scholarship. For example, I've been writing about the Nanih Waiya, the Choctaw's Mother Mound for the last twenty years. For thousands of years, Choctaws were mound builders. Six years ago, a group of performance artists, myself included, received a Social Sciences and Humanities Research Council grant to study mounds throughout the Western Hemisphere. We visited and researched eighteen mound sites, and that research material will be performed in our new play, *Sideshow Freaks and Circus Injuns*. What began as a story in my novel and short stories grew into a large research project and now a new play, cowritten by Monique Mojica and me, with many cocreators from southeastern tribes in the US. It's a large cast.

RM: Do you see yourself as responding to a Native American literary tradition—either in terms of tribal storytelling traditions or to what has been called the Native American Renaissance?

LH: I don't worry about labels or how academics want to situate our work as Native/Indigenous writers. I write what interests me at the time. I have a new book of poetry, and I've just finished a book on Mary Todd Lincoln and a Dakota Indian called *Savage Conversations*. I really don't worry about labels. Writers worry about syntax, voice, setting or landscape, plot, and the arc of the story. We worry about craft, the art of the writing.

RM: When we met at NALS, one of the main things I took away is how inherently intertwined scholarship and activism are in this community. Academia needs to have practical and tangible relevance for Indigenous communities—and this is something you deal with in your novel *Shell Shaker*, through Auda's work as a historian. How do you see the relationship between academia and activism?

LH: Writing is a form of activism. Again, let's not separate into small boxes activism versus writing. Native people, I think, prefer to think in more holistic terms. A story is active, and a story changes the world. A story is changing the world as I write this.

RM: Thinking about this in relation to the current political climate in the US, I wonder how you see Native communities and authors responding to the issues that are unfolding.

LH: I'm not sure how to answer this. How are white, Black, Asian writers responding to the political climate in the US? It's hard to say—that is my point. I have a new poem, "Gatorland," coming out in *Bullets into Bells: Poets and Citizens Respond to Gun Violence in the US* (Fall 2017). This new anthology is edited by Brian Clements, Alexandra Teague, and Dean Rader and has the star power of poetic greats—I'm not talking about myself. I also have new poems in another anthology: *Truth to Power: Writers Respond to the Rhetoric of Hate and Fear* (Spring 2017) edited by Pamela Uschuk. My new novel that I'm working on is about the Arab Revolt in 1917 and Arab Spring in 2011, with Choctaws involved in both those events. I write about issues and events that have taken place in the past but resonate with the present. At least, they do for me.

Writers, in general, always respond to the politics of oppression, race, class, gender, and so on. I'm probably more interested in the question of how tribes are responding to the politics of oppression. In October 2017, my tribe sent a group of Choctaws to the Standing Rock Sioux Tribe in North Dakota to lend support to Dakota Sioux people protesting the Dakota Access Pipeline that would go beneath the Missouri River. The Choctaws gave thousands of dollars' worth of supplies, lanterns, sleeping bags, propane heaters, and tents to Standing Rock. This act of tribal generosity speaks for itself against acts of tyranny, whether by corporations or governments. Many other tribes around the US sent aid to Standing Rock last year. If we extrapolate backwards, this is an example of why tribes were so deeply connected to one another before the arrival of immigrants in the fifteenth century. These examples offer a different view of ancient and historical cooperation among tribes, not warfare.

RM: In your writing, you have explored historical instances of transnational exchange and cooperation, particularly with relation to the donation the Choctaws made to the Irish in the nineteenth century. Do you see this kind of solidarity as having the potential to counteract some of the issues facing our global society?

LH: I wish I believed that. The Cherokees, Creeks, and some Choctaws supported the fledgling US and Andrew Jackson's forces in warfare against the British in 1812–1815. It didn't keep our tribes from being removed by Jackson's government from our homelands. Alas.

RM: To finish, you have spoken and written previously about the power of Native stories—your theory of tribalography explores their transformative capacity. Do you feel that telling stories can help to redress power imbalances?

LH: Perhaps. But there will always be more work to accomplish. Growing readers is a major concern for all of us. In the beginning of my career, there were fewer Native writers. Thankfully, that has changed. Right now, on my nightstand, there are two newly published books I'm reading by Ojibwe writers: Carter Meland's *Stories for a Lost Child* and Heid Erdrich's *Curator of Ephemera at the New Museum for Archaic Media*. Both are terrific. However, I meet people all the time who say they have never heard of people like Louise Erdrich, Vine Deloria, Susan Power, Natalie Diaz, Joy Harjo, Daniel Heath Justice, and Ernestine Hayes—Native writers who are alive and well in the universe and creating new books of fiction, poetry, and creative nonfiction. We are still a vacant map as Native writers of Native literature. But a story chooses a writer, not the other way around. I believe we write, perform, *because we must*. Nothing else is of importance. Native writers will grow and develop as the stories search them out. That's exciting, and the stories will change the world.

Rebecca Macklin is a postgraduate tutor and PhD candidate in comparative literature at the University of Leeds. Her research is focused on Native American and South African contemporary fiction.

"An American in New York": LeAnne Howe

Kirstin L. Squint / 2019

Unpublished interview conducted October 9, 2019. Published by permission of Kirstin L. Squint.

On October 8, 2019, Kirstin L. Squint and LeAnne Howe met in New York City to attend a performance of *Savage Conversations* at the Ensemble Studio Theatre at 549 West 52nd Street. The performance was adapted from Howe's play in verse *Savage Conversations* (Coffee House Press, 2019), which tells the story of Mary Todd Lincoln's addiction to opiates in 1875 and the Indian ghost that she claimed tormented her. The reading was dramatized by members of the Ensemble Studio Theatre, directed by Paul Austin. The interview followed on October 9 over coffee and rolls.[1]

Kirstin L. Squint: Let's start with beginnings. In *Choctalking on Other Realities*, especially in the Prologue and in "Carlos Castaneda Lives in Romania," you address your relationship with your birth mother and your adopted mother, which you also do, to an extent, in the documentary *Indian Country Diaries: Spiral of Fire*. Can you tell the story of your birth and how the relationships you had with your mothers impacted you as a mother and as a writer?

LeAnne Howe: I was born in a home for unwed mothers in Edmond, Oklahoma. Ten or fifteen years ago, maybe longer, I went back there to look at the place, and it had become a restaurant. Which I think is funny. Instead of something like "I was born in a hospital" or "I was born on a farm," I can truthfully say I was born in a restaurant. But there's more. At the time I was born, it was also connected to a movie house, and I would like to think that—and I have said this before—playing on the big screen was a Western, some kind of cowboy and Indian film starring John Wayne. I don't know what was showing because I couldn't find out. But Mother left me shortly after she had me. Later I learned I was there for another five days before I was adopted. [During that time] I was just in the care of nurses, and I don't think there was anyone around except for nurses during feeding times. I don't think they starved me or that kind of thing. I was in a home for unwed mothers for five days by myself, and I think that experience of being left in the care of nurses or whomever instilled a feeling of abandonment in me. I don't think it; I know it. That's a thing I've had to work against, this need to be running, running, running, running away. You know, being alone. I was surrounded by other Indian babies in similar circumstances, I suppose. I know that, for the baby that was born there before me, one of the nurses or the doctors put the wrong kind of solution in the baby's eyes [and the solution] blinded it. I guess I'm thankful that I can see, but this place was a home for unwed mothers. It was poor, it was charity, it was negligence, so I think the feeling that I've had all my life is that I have to run, to get away, get away, get away. When my adopted mother came for me five days later, she took me to Ada, Oklahoma, to my grandmother's house. You know, that also anchored a sense of stability in me because I now own that house. I've remodeled it, and it is the first home I had, literally, and it will be the last home that I have, so therein is the circle. But it is still a history of feeling abandoned. I also think I must have been a real hellion. My adoptive mother was frustrated with me, I know that. She didn't know how to take care of a baby, and she was exasperated. When I was a little kid, she always threatened to take me back to the orphanage, take me back to the house where I was born. "If you don't straighten up, I'm going to take you to the orphanage!" And finally I thought, although I didn't know the word at the time, "Well, fuck, I will run away before you can." And I remember that the anger I had as a little kid was from that threat: "Pack your clothes, I'm going to take you back to the home!" You know? And so those two things coupled together probably helped me become a better writer. A person who was able to resist. "I hate all of you": that's the kind of mantra I go to when I'm in an uncomfortable situation. "I hate all of you people here," but you learn how not to show it, right? And that's a kind of pain that I've tried as a writer to write through. It's probably the reason I became a writer: to determine the internal dialogue of my characters, versus the "what I will show" to people who read the stories. I would say that my childhood was not particularly happy; those were brutal times and also the reason I would run away. When recess was on, I would run away from school. That running away pattern has probably only stopped in the last few years. Most of my life has been spent trying to run away. Running is also the underlying pain many of my characters carry with them in my novels and short fiction.

KLS: I've read some different things about your tribal background, so I just wanted to clarify—your birth mother was Choctaw, and you were adopted by a Cherokee woman. Is that right?

LH: A Cherokee family, yes. But I also knew my Choctaw birth name and later my aunts and uncles. My birth mother took me to meet them. They were very welcoming to me.

KLS: And then, your grandmother at the home in Ada was Choctaw?

LH: No, she's my Cherokee grandma in Ada.

KLS: And then your father was Cherokee?

LH: My father was Cherokee, but I never met him. That was the story my birth mother told me: "Well, your dad was Cherokee. He had coal black hair."

KLS: I have written about you as a southern writer, and we have talked a lot about southeastern tribes including the Cherokees and the Choctaws and their land in the South. Do you identify as Choctaw because you were born Choctaw? But you have had Cherokee cultural experiences—I don't even know how to talk about this; it seems bigger than that. Can you talk about that? I mean you wouldn't identify as Cherokee because Choctaws are matrilineal. But how would you describe your relationship to Cherokee culture, or the Nation, given your position of being adopted into it, I mean literally adopted in?

LH: Well, I identify as Choctaw because my [birth] mother was Choctaw. And Granny, my adopted grandmother, [who was Cherokee,] would say, "Oh, you're not one of us, but we love you, we wanted you." [The documentary] *The Spiral of Fire* was kind of a happenstance because I'm there to interview Cherokee people in the Eastern Band, and *The Spiral of Fire* is about those connections, so it becomes, towards the end of the film, "You know, my dad was Cherokee, but I'm not Cherokee." And I'm not confused about this. And even the Eastern Band Cherokee people that I talked to, off or on camera, would say, "Yeah, but you're not one of us." I think it comes through in the film, you know. And I'm a self-soother. But I am not Cherokee, and I never met my father, and that was my own fault because my birth mother said, "I'll take you to meet your dad." He was still alive when she offered to introduce me. He probably died in the mid-1990s. In fact, she called me; I was teaching at Carlton College when he died. She called and told me, "Well, he's dead." Just like that. "Who died? Oh no!" "Your Dad," she said. At that moment I realized, and she certainly never told me, that she'd kept up with him all those years. She kept up with what happened to him because he always lived in McAlester. I think that my birth was always embarrassing to her. It's understandable. Think of her generation. This is my birth mother again. She was embarrassed that she had me, and that's the reason she abandoned me. She didn't want anybody to know that she had had me. And then I came marching back into her life, and she had never expected to see me.

KLS: How old were you then?

LH: Um, let's see, probably in my mid-twenties, something like that because I had children. It must have been somewhere between twenty-four or twenty-five because I had my two sons, too. I was nineteen and twenty-one when my sons were born. So it was probably in my mid-twenties, maybe older, somewhere back there. Mother had never expected that I would come back like a bad penny. But she took it well and tried to fill in all the years of her life and my life by weaving me together with my uncles and aunts. She took me into the family. My uncles knew I was born but didn't know what she had done with me. People were glad I was back, and so it's awesome. I have a huge family. Joe and Randy [my sons] were little, and my Choctaw family took us in like, "Wow, we're so glad you're back!" [*Laughs*]

KLS: Wow, that's a lot to deal with.

LH: Yes, it was. Then on the other side of the family, my Cherokee family, the interesting thing to me, and I didn't put this together until many years later, is that my Great Grandma Hatton was Cherokee, but she was also a little bit Chickasaw. We found out many, many, years after she died. Isn't that interesting? We didn't know that for decades. Granny's grandfather, Grandma Hatton's father was a full-blood Cherokee. You know I hate to bring up "blood quantum," but he was a full blood, so that lineage is there. They ended up in Oklahoma. Great Grandma Hatton was born around 1879, Granny was born in 1898. They are coming from the east through Van Buren, Arkansas. I don't think they're necessarily part of the Removal Era, but it takes them into the 1870s to get into Indian Territory. That migration of that family is not necessarily unlike the Choctaws, who were also pushed out of their homelands and ended up in Indian Territory. Both of those communities in my family—my Cherokee "fictive kin," to use a term by anthropologists, came through my adoption, and the Choctaws in my bloodline—are both coming out of the east, settling in and around McAlester. And the Cherokee family had been in Van Buren until they came into the Stonewall area. As a young person, I couldn't have made these linking connections. But Ada's the first home I ever had. Mother abandoned me, and so that explains the importance of home in *Choctalking*, but it is also part of *Miko Kings*. That house, that home, that birthplace. You know, it's not my birthplace, but it's my birth home. And I have a picture of myself with my Cherokee grandmother holding me out in front of her like a basket. I'm five or six days old. I don't think it's unlike other people's stories, per se, but that's the story of my beginnings. It also explains the abandonment themes in my work, and the feeling of home that Lena has and needs when she remodels her house in *Miko Kings*. Lena has been living in the Middle East, and she's come home to make the house in Ada her home, all the while knowing it is filled with ghosts. I remodeled my grandmother's house knowing it is filled with the ghosts of family. I also found my grandfather's letters that he had been writing to a little girl, and she was fourteen and living in Kentucky.

KLS: You found those when you were remodeling the house?

LH: Yeah, he had hidden them.

KLS: [*Laughs*] Oh my God, so that pouch in the wall in *Miko Kings* is real?

LH: It's true, it's true! The walls were lath and plaster, so we're knocking those out to put in sheet rock, and that's when they found the letters. The stamps are really rare, and the fact is my grandfather had been writing this girl, and she wrote back letters to him, and we have both of those because she sent them back on the same paper. The other interesting thing is when I found the letters, or I didn't find them, the two guys who were knocking the plaster out of the walls found them. Chelsey, my granddaughter, and Alyssa are with me, and I'm driving the three of us from Ada to Austin, Texas, to see my brother. Chelsey, who's got to be eight or nine at the time, is reading the letters back to me as I'm driving, and then she stops reading. She's a little kid, and she says, "Wait a minute, I don't think this girl was Granny." And [*chuckling*] I said, "No, it can't be Granny." Now here's the thing: she'd never met Granny. She only knows of Granny from my stories, and I laughed and laughed and laughed. I thought, "Wow, that's how storytelling works. It's power. She's talking about Granny like she knew her." But Granny had died in the 1980s; Chelsey had never met her, but she talked like she knew her. That's the power of stories and how they are carried on. Anyway, the letters my grandfather kept in the walls of the house were from his teenage years long before he met and married my Cherokee grandmother. He was her second husband because her first husband had died in the 1918 pandemic.

KLS: I was going to ask you about *Miko Kings* and the relationship of the characters to your own identity. LeAnne Howe is a pseudonym.

LH: [*Chuckles*] That's right. Izola is my first name.

KLS: Can you talk about when and why you started using a pseudonym and how it affects your day-to-day life? Also, Ezol's and Lena's names are so similar to your own. I just taught the novel, and I was remembering that Ezol is like *isolé* in French, isolated or isolation. I want to know about your pseudonym's impact on you, but also, were Ezol and Lena sides of yourself when you were writing them? I mean obviously there's some stuff with the house in Ada that I didn't realize was so connected to your experience.

LH: I want to say that I started using pseudonyms when I was in my twenties, and I think it goes back to being abandoned, self-soothing, running away. I had three or four pseudonyms on the mailbox in Stillwater, Oklahoma. Sheila was one of the names I used. I had started to invent new identities, and I put all those different names on the mailbox at the house that we rented. Sheree was my roommate, and we shared a house while taking classes at OSU. Sheree Turner is a dear friend with whom I am still in touch, and I love her dearly. But we lived together, and she is probably the only undergraduate, eighteen- or nineteen-year-old, who would have moved in with Joe and Randy and me. She had names on the mailbox too, and she was a hippie. Even though hippie culture was waning, she was still a hippie, and we had pseudonyms that we used to write away for magazines. I would put a different name on the mailbox, so I could get different free magazines. I started writing under all these same names, and Sheila Willing was one name I remember because I thought it was hilarious. Sherry's van that we rode around in and she would take the boys to school in was named "So What" after one of Joe Walsh's albums. [*Squint laughs.*] I mean, it had huge letters that she and her brother had painted on, so you could see it coming. The pseudonyms to me are just another extension of self-soothing, and I thought it was funny just like lots of lines in my plays that are asides, that I think are funny, and some of them are inside jokes, but they're all about the same thing. Running away, making fun, and making fun of. Kinda of like the humor that's in *Miko Kings*, funny and tragic. Also, I've wondered about my own stability, especially as a younger person and having [what was called at the time] Asperger's syndrome. I'm no doctor, so I may not know what I'm talking about. These are the thoughts that one keeps to oneself—until this interview.

KLS: So you wrote that into Ezol Day's character? She has Asperger's syndrome.

LH: Mmm-hmm. Yeah. Yeah. And the ability to concentrate so hard on what you're doing that you miss everything around you. My sons would say that's absolutely part of my personality. I have an ability to block out everything. It's also the same ability that helps me rename myself and every so often block out the past, pull a new name out of the air, and put it on the mailbox. That's another element of being a self-soother; there is a bit of narcissism in that. I'm well aware of that, too.

KLS: I think that it's different if you take that and you turn it into art versus, you know, negative possibilities.

LH: I hope so! [*Laughs*]

KLS: It's creative!

LH: I definitely hope so!

[*Both laughing*]

KLS: Wow, that's really interesting. I guess this is kind of like a logistical question that I am interested in with pseudonyms because I think about this a lot, weirdly enough I guess. Does your family call you LeAnne? Have you used it for more of your life than any other name? Is LeAnne actually part of your name?

LH: Yeah, it is.

KLS: Okay.

LH: Izola was my adopted mother's name, and she decided to give it to me—though I know she didn't like her name and I hate it. But she called me LeAnne, never Izola. And then she was a Lynch at the time, so that's what's on my birth certificate.

KLS: I see.

LH: I actually have two birth certificates. One is the Billy girl, and that's my first birth certificate. I was a Billy girl, no father. Christine Billy is my birth mother. I had to go to court to get the original birth certificate and then open up my adoption papers. Then the next birth certificate is when I am named. So, for me the pseudonyms are no different from having all these transitional names at different periods of my life. And look at the way in which names change throughout our lives. Especially as women. We don't change our names anymore, but the older tradition was that women would change their names for each husband they married. So, for me, it just seems like something natural that is a pattern. "Well, I'll just change my name." For each name change, I've become a different person. This is a process I use when I'm developing the characters I'm working on. For instance, in *Shell Shaker*, Auda is my sister's name.

KLS: Oh! And the characters are Billys.

LH: Yes.

KLS: Thank you. The pseudonym has been a burning question of mine for some time.

LH: Really?!

KLS: Yeah! I don't know why I never asked you before! So, in the past, we have talked a lot about Choctaws and your relationship with the Southeast. Today I would love to hear you talk about Oklahoma, which you have been doing already. How did being born and raised in Oklahoma shape you as a writer, and what is your relationship to Oklahoma, the land and the people today?

LH: I think of myself as an Oklahoman because I was born there. I think of myself as a Choctaw because I am Choctaw, that's my birth family, that's the Billys. That's who I am, and that's where they live. They're mostly in and around McAlester, some around Tannehill outside of McAlester. I think of myself as having the same histories as they had. Embodied histories, right? Even my Cherokee family. They all lived through the Dust Bowl, so those experiences shaped them and, by extension, me, through the stories that are passed down, even though the southeastern part of the state wasn't hit as hard as other parts of the state. Oklahoma's Dust Bowl happened to people who were out west and in Texas and so forth, but certainly, it happened to my families, both sides. There are a few stories Granny told about having to put wet rags on the edge of her windowsills when the dust was blowing too fiercely. She talked about, during the Dust Bowl, having to put a wet rag over her face to go outside because the air was so soupy with gritty sand. So that happened, and I can tell that story, but it didn't happen to me. It's exactly like the story I told of Chelsey and the letters she read in the car going to Austin. She didn't know my grandmother, but she called out her name "Granny" like she knew her. I passed down those stories to the next generation. We embody and know these stories during the Dust Bowl about being so poor that you don't know where the next meal will come from. I know those stories. When I look at the pictures of my adopted family from that era, they are all about as big around as my little finger. They are thin and stringy-looking. I look like my Choctaw aunts, and the whole Billy family, we are a little chunky. But in those pictures of my Choctaw aunts and my mother in that same era, they are all skin and bones. It's from not getting enough calories every day. And so, this Indian place, coming into what will become "Indian Territory" for them, I didn't experience that sorrow, but I feel like I did. I know the stories. I am gifted with Oklahoma stories, with Removal stories, with *my God*, extreme poverty stories. When, as a little kid, I stayed with Granny in Ada, we would walk to town, and there would be the pencil man on the sidewalk. He had no legs and was selling pencils because he was homeless. He was living by the railroad because by that time the railroad came through. How he lost his legs we didn't know, but we would go by him and drop a couple pennies into his rusted coffee can. And not take the pencils. Then we would go from store to store in Ada. The Russians ran the shoe store. There was a Lebanese tailor in downtown Ada. There was a Chinese laundry in Ada. Why? Because Ada was a railroad town. My grandfather worked at the feed mill; that's why he contracted emphysema that eventually killed him. The Nazarene Church that he and my grandmother attended on their block was on the corner of 9th Street and Oak Street. I have vivid memories of this place, and this town, because I walked that landscape with my grandmother and was introduced to all the people that she knew. They were people who had lived their lives in and around Pontotoc County. And they were also very thin and pretty poor. I feel like that's Oklahoma legacy to Indian people. The nation-state, the greed of settlers didn't kill them, but nearly did. And you know as a little kid I'm dark; I have long black hair. We went to school in Oklahoma City, in Bethany, in Moore, and around Oklahoma City, and my grade school teachers at the time would say, "Who's the little Indian princess?" Thinking back on it now, I see that was really hard and ironic. There's a lot that was hard. My adopted mother married an insane man. He tried to kill us all. He ended up drinking Drano in the backyard one summer's day, right after he tried to stab her. After he drank Drano, he was sent to Norman and diagnosed with homicidal schizophrenia.[2] Maybe he went crazy as a soldier in World War II; maybe he didn't. But the point is he tried to kill us, tried to kill me several times, and finally he was put in Norman in a mental institution, and he died.

KLS: Is that when you were a child?

LH: Yeah! By the time I was eleven years old, maybe twelve, I'd already had to fight him off me, as he was trying to stab me with a knife in the house. He broke out of Norman several times trying to get back to us. These are all events that are collapsing now in time, but the three of us—my adopted brother, my adoptive mom, and me—slept together on a foldout bed in the living room for at least a year after he was institutionalized because he would break out, come home with a knife, and try to kill us. So, this was part of my childhood. The first thing you learn or the first thing *I* learned was to run.

KLS: Yeah.

LH: Eventually we sold that house and moved to Midwest City, but running was the thing that I knew how to do. And when I was terrified, I would lock the door, and we would sleep on the couch because that would be the way that we would hear him and defend ourselves. We could run out the back and run away. In *Choctalking*, there is a run, run, run, refrain in the fiction and memoir. Run away from people who were calling us names, calling me names. And that's the story of Oklahoma—The Great Run.

KLS: I want to dig into this a little more. That's where you're from, where so much of your writing comes from. I was recently in Oklahoma and talked to a lot of people who love and admire your work. Today you are a renowned Oklahoma writer, so what is that like? Especially given that much of your professional life has not been in Oklahoma, even though you own a home and go back there regularly. How is it to come home and be a writer doing events, mentoring writers, all of the things that you do, as an Oklahoman?

LH: I don't think Oklahomans pay much attention to what we do, but rather who we are. I'm someone's neighbor and family, that kind of thing.

KLS: Okay.

LH: You know I think this is the story of Oklahoma. The insider and outsider of the story. I'm doing a collection of poems with Dean Rader, also from Oklahoma, where we are writing every other poem in the book. It's call and response writing. He's an Oklahoma writer, but he's from the western part of the state, Weatherford. But what is inside-outside? We haven't yet defined in the poetry what makes Oklahoma an inside-outside place. But it will be there in the poetry. Maybe it's the weather and what we are able to mask. As we are writers, I hope it will be revealed in the poetry. That's what we're aiming towards. We've been working on this quite a while since we started writing back and forth, so I want to wrap it up in 2020 if we can. Those poems haven't come out yet. How do you write as an Oklahoman with all of the trappings of terror? It was a terrifying childhood. But the mask that I put on as a child was of being quiet. You know, the "chew off your arm type before revealing any emotion," that kind of a thing, and just keep going.

KLS: What you were saying about the stories that you have inside of you, like Indian Removal, makes me think of *Miko Kings*—I just taught it, so I've been thinking about it a lot. Even that main character is running. There are scenes of running and not wanting to go home and then going home to Oklahoma.

LH: Kinda crazy!

KLS: Yeah, and Indian Territory is overlaid or underlaid. It's happening stickily in that piece. It exists, they exist simultaneously, and I think that's interesting because that's the way you just talked about it.

LH: Yeah, yeah. And trying to unwind it especially in *Miko Kings* when Lena comes home. You know she's happily lived abroad, and I know what that's like because I lived in Jordan. It feels like super freedom, being really free of my past, and I can be anyone. Lost in crowds of black-haired people,

I'd never felt such happiness. Odd to say. But living there was like being out of a straitjacket. But of course, we carry the same emotions whenever we go. Here's what I do think. I'm probably a very typical Oklahoman with the same inside-outside story. You know, Oklahoma is a mean little place. It's also a beloved place. So, how do you negotiate those identities and think that I'm similarly negotiating inside-outside? I'm likely very similar to most Oklahomans. Maybe that's emblematic of a larger America because, I mean, look! America is very much a story of call and response, murdering Native Americans, stealing their land, and run, run, and run, we're still being murdered. Chances are we live alone with our murderers. Terrifying. Think of the over 5,712 missing and murdered Native women in 2016. That's a fact, and those numbers are three years old. And that too is the story of America.

KLS: Indeed. It's horrifying. This idea of complex relationships to place also applies to your relationship with the South, which we have talked about a great deal in past conversations. You've been working at the University of Georgia for five years now, right?

LH: Going on six—this is my sixth year!

KLS: Wow! Previously we have talked a lot about the Choctaws' homelands in the South, so to follow up on that, I'm wondering how you think of your current relationship to the South in terms of teaching there and being a southeastern Native woman living in the Southeast.

LH: You know I think that my relationship to the South and to Georgia, but also Mississippi and all the states in between, has been a process of digging in. That's kind of a metaphor related to Choctaw mound culture and mound cities. Our homelands are replete with mounds. The Choctaws built Nanih Waiya in Mississippi, which I have been to many times. It's easy to get to. The mound in plain sight—she's right there hiding in plain sight in Winston County, Mississippi. It's emblematic of Indians when you think about it. We're hiding in plain sight. My aunts returned to our birth mound. I'm not sure that Mother ever did return to Nanih Waiya. I used to run back and forth between Oklahoma and Nanih Waiya, so in that way I'm just retracing what my aunts did, what many of the Billys did. I know my cousins went to Mississippi to look at our birth mound and our homelands, where we'd come from as a people before Indian Removal. In that way, I am returning. I'm constantly returning. I started a series at the University of Georgia called American Indian Returnings, AIR Talks. We hosted Sarah Deer in 2019. Previously, in other years, we've hosted for AIR Talks Jodi Byrd, Joy Harjo, Daniel Justice, and Chadwick Allen, all southeastern Natives or descendants. Jodi Byrd, Chickasaw and professor at the University of Illinois, was the first lecturer in the American Indian Returnings series. I'm trying to show through this series that we Natives are returning to the land that we were torn away from, a place we had to abandon. To make that circle again, one of the things that I've done at the University of Georgia is to bring back Native scholars and writers into that territory, into that place. Native scholars and poets for AIR have lectured on the idea of returnings. In my mind, however crazed I am, all of this works in the same way. It's about coming back, circling back to the places where we were taken from, whether by choice or at the point of a gun. We are returning. Georgia has offered me a great opportunity to be in the South, to be a part of the intellectual landscape of the Southeast. As a Native, to be able to teach, create curriculum, and bring other Natives to Georgia around this idea of returning has been a great joy. I'm focusing on returnings in Native literature in the class that I'm teaching this semester, trying to instill in graduate students that sense of land and landscape, how important it is. You know, I am really, really driven by the kind of Native themes I can bring to mainstream students. Hopefully, I will have influenced students and others to continue looking at the ways in which southeastern Natives are returning to our birthplace. That's what the University of Georgia offers me, and I'm grateful. Jace Weaver [Director of the Institute of Native American Studies at the university] reached out to me when this position was opening in the English Department. I'm very grateful that he did and for his support going through the process of being hired at Georgia because, to me, being here represents return.

KLS: Georgia has such a terrible history in terms of Indian Removal, and it's a very good thing that the University of Georgia wants to do that and have Indigenous southeastern literature be part of the curriculum and events, so I am so thrilled you are there.

LH: Thank you, Kirstin, for asking about it.

KLS: This reminds me of another burning question I have had for some time. When you came to High Point University to speak back in 2014, you told the audience at your reading that you spent ten years researching *Shell Shaker*, which is, of course, partially set in the eighteenth-century Southeast. Can you talk about the research process for that book or about your research process more broadly?

LH: When I say that I spent ten years researching *Shell Shaker*, there was a lot more to it. I researched the Newberry Library's Ayers collection and its Karpinski Collection of maps, so I could trace the Choctaw movements on those older French maps. I went to the Smithsonian Institution for a month-long intern fellowship that Rayna Green administered. I was looking into

the archives for Cyrus Byington's files to see how he took some of the meanings of our original words and shoehorned them into Biblical phrases with
Biblical meanings. That was how he was subtly changing the nuances of our
language. And then teaching it to small Choctaw children captured by the
missionaries. They were away from their parents for the entire school year.

In other words, I always thought that there were many layers of Choctaw discourse: one for household speakers, one for traders—Mabila is one
example—and one level for diplomats. But something was missing. I con-
cluded, rightly or wrongly, that there was another layer of language that the
Choctaw philosophers and Diviners used: things that the average person
didn't speak of. For example, you can see philosophy and/or spirituality in
all the terms relating to blood or bone picking. In all those eighteenth-
century speakers and speeches that a Choctaw speaker would use in council, there were words spoken for a Chief to the French or Spanish in council.[3]

KLS: I know that you recently attended the inaugural reading by US Poet
Laureate Joy Harjo, the first Native American in this position. What does it
mean to you that Joy Harjo has been named US poet laureate?

LH: Oh, my gosh! What does it mean to me that Joy Harjo is the first
Native poet laureate? I was elated. I'm just elated for the recognition of her
work. This is a powerful moment in our history—as Native writers and as
Native people. This Indigenous spirit has been building in her work for centuries. I was so happy to see the culmination of her work at her inaugural
poetry reading in Washington, DC. The reading happened at what I call the
mouth of the lion, a place that has devoured Native people over the centuries: Washington, DC. She was returning women's powerful voices as the first
Native US poet laureate, and being there was one of the epic moments of my
life. It was absolutely extraordinary, and I couldn't be happier. I got there the
day of the reading and met with Mvskoke/Creek poet Jennifer Foerster as well
as Owen Sapulpa, Joy's husband. Joy's children were there, and it was just a
glorious, glorious event. I could see, at the Library of Congress, the women
who work there were all very celebratory and accommodating. Joy, Jennifer,
and I had just turned in the first draft of the manuscript for *When the Light
of the World Was Subdued, Our Songs Came Through: A Norton Anthology
of Native Nations Poetry* (2020). The anthology contains some one hundred
and sixty Native poets, representing over a hundred Indigenous nations. The
culmination of that editing work coincided with Joy's inaugural reading as
US poet laureate. Her reading that night was the best I've ever heard her. So
powerful, joyful—to put her name in that word—and extraordinary. And
one of the moments that stands out of editing the manuscript is the three of

us reading aloud Eleazar's "Elegy," which was written in 1678 when he was one of the Harvard Indians.[4] In the editing process, the three of us would read aloud each and every one of these poems to make sure they were correct on the page. Speaking their names, as well as pulling the earliest work we could find that would fit in the anthology, was overwhelming. We could feel the ancestors of poetry were with us in this process. Isn't that exciting?

KLS: That is *so* exciting.

LH: It's amazing, and it represents, again back to our own work, a culmination of studied but also lived experiences.

KLS: Oh, my heart just sang when I heard the news. And I want to thank you all for the work. This anthology is so needed. I can't wait to see it.

LH: It's got a long title: *When the Light of the World Was Subdued, Our Songs Came Through: A Norton Anthology of Native Nations Poetry.*

KLS: On other exciting topics, last night we got to see the first staged reading of *Savage Conversations* at Ensemble Studio Theater in New York City. It was an amazing performance. Before we get into any specifics about the play, can you just talk about the experience of seeing the dramatic reading of it?

LH: You were there [*laughs*], but I don't think—I hope that it didn't show—I was shaking all over. By the time they get to one of those scenes of really explosive power between Mary Todd Lincoln and Savage Indian—you know there's this tension between them that the director Paul Austin really pulled out of the actors. All the power of the Savage Indian and Mary's madness was manifested onstage. My physical body, my heart, my whole body was shaking because I'm on fire the way the performers are on fire. Even my organs were shaking all over because I was thinking, "Oh, my God, they got it." They got exactly what I saw and felt as I was writing the play, and I don't think that happens often. Although maybe it does.

KLS: I don't think so.

LH: It was a tremendous moment to see really good actors on stage, doing what you envision as a writer. What a privilege. I owe a debt of gratitude to Paul Austin and the Ensemble Studio Theatre.

KLS: I'm so glad I was there for that.

LH: Me too. I'm so glad you were there with me because it was a lot of fun, and these moments don't come around often. I'm so happy you've taken an interest in my work. Thank you.

KLS: It was a lot of fun!

LH: It was really, I don't know, epic! It felt epic for me to see the work because when I was writing the story, it was emotional work. You know, in a way, the story has its roots in my own adopted father's mental insanity. That's what happens to Mary. Because of her insanity, she wants her body to be mutilated every night. Who would think of such a thing but a madwoman. Really what Mary Todd Lincoln wanted was to be cut. It's what she tells the doctors. She wants to be cut up at night.

KLS: What made you decide to draw together her insanity with the hanging of the Dakota 38? As you said, in her journals this savage Indian visited her nightly, but what made you decide to make him one of the Dakota thirty-eight?

LH: That's the only thing it could be, right? I don't think I did that. I think that was what was haunting Mary. I do believe she felt haunted; otherwise, why would she be haunted by a Native? And you know in Lexington, Kentucky, there aren't many Indians living in that city when she's born. She was raised in a privileged household. She goes to a boarding school where she learns to speak French. There aren't any Indians there. Not that I could find in the historic records. Yes, Natives were in Kentucky, of course, but it can't be.

KLS: She wasn't coming into contact with tribes like she might have been were she in—

LH: North Carolina?

KLS: Right.

LH: But the kind of Native that she imagines is certainly not the Cherokees.

KLS: Right.

LH: And when I read her insanity file, I believed it must be the Dakotas she was imagining, because that's the event that she would have known of in 1862. And look what happens: Lincoln is shot in the head. And the Dakotas were hanged by the head, well, the neck, I mean. To my way of thinking, Mary's insanity grows after the thirty-eight Dakota were hanged.

KLS: You mentioned you've been thinking about doing some more work on Mary Todd Lincoln?

LH: Yes.

KLS: What more would you explore? I was thinking last night that she's very different from most of the central characters of your works. They're usually Choctaw. Where would you go if you continued writing about her?

LH: I'm shocked too, because I have spent most of my literary career writing about Choctaws. Both of the characters in *Savage Conversations* came to me; I wasn't searching them out. I think he appeared to me first. Savage Indian. She called him an "Indian ghost," but the savagery that happens to her face is exactly what she wrote about and talked about with her doctors. In her dreams she is mutilated, which is a savage act. I didn't choose to do a story about them; that story chose me. I never, ever, ever, ever write about another tribe, so I had to think about this for a while. But he came first; his voice came first. I read the insanity file and *pffft*. He came right in, so I had to do it. I had to follow that. I talked to my dear, dear friend Susan Power about this, again and again, and she gave me permission to follow my instincts.[5] She gave me the strength to do it. I talked to Susan about this, and then I had given a reading before the book came out at Bemidji where there were Dakota writers in the audience. No one had any concerns. I tried to be as careful as I could be with the event itself, but it had to be the power of that event that was so frightening and pulled me to it. In the end, the story is about Mary Todd Lincoln and the Dakota thirty-eight.

KLS: I want to wrap up with just one last question that also pertains to *Savage Conversations*. In your body of work, you have this series of poems about Noble Savage in *Evidence of Red*, and Noble Savage has come up in other works, and then, of course, this Savage Indian comes from Mary Todd Lincoln's journals. Do you see "savagery" operating in different ways in this text? I mean this is one of those colonial binaries, right? This word gets attached to Indigenous peoples, so it's one that a lot of Indigenous folks have tried to work through and tried to deconstruct. Is that what you're doing? The Noble Savage poems are very funny, and there's some humor in this play and of course a lot of violence, too. I'm not sure I'm making my point . . .

LH: No, keep going.

KLS: I'm really just working through this after seeing the staged reading last night. I guess what I'm wondering is: do you see the savagery as being similar in these pieces, and is there a difference in the sort of tongue-in-cheek Rousseauian Noble Savage of your poetry and this Savage Indian that Mary Todd Lincoln has conjured?

LH: Oh, wow, that's a difficult question. Let me clear up something now. In Mary Todd Lincoln's talk with Dr. Danforth, she calls the ghost an "Indian spirit," and it's the acts she describes that are brutal and savage so that's what I was reacting to. She blames Indian people for her insanity and the brutality she so desires to happen to her.

KLS: Oh, I see.

LH: I put "savage" in the Mary Todd Lincoln story because I have always used savage as a trope. I am actually very proud to be called a "savage Indian" by the people who brought genocide to Natives. Or slavery, or any number of holocausts. So look out here, as a savage I might fuck you up, and that's my bravado as a writer and a performer. That was what Roxy Gordon and I were writing in our first play, *Big PowWow*. The old ghost in that play was not like my Noble Savage in later poetry, such as the animation "Noble Savage Learns to Tweet,"[6] but I've always thought of us as the people "who tracked every trace of this world." I'm quoting Susan Power here. We were the people that brought the world medicines like aspirin and many other curatives. And Natives propagated indigenous plants that would feed the whole goddam planet, and yet we were called savages. How fucked up is that? I've always played with this notion of Native as savage, including in my latest work, *Savage Conversations*. "Savage Indian" is the civilizing effect on this crazy uncivilized woman, Mary Todd Lincoln. She gets better because of him. In effect, and here is the hubris, this land, this country is America because of American Indians.

KLS: Absolutely.

LH: So, Savage Indian is the intellectual center of *Savage Conversations*. And yeah, he's funny, and at the same time, he is capable of saying, "Look out, I will fuck you up." Yet, he never says that. But you know I do [*laughs*].

KLS: But he does force Mary to be honest with herself.

LH: Yeah, and he keeps brow-beating her like a counselor or psychiatrist might. The same kind of theme is in the Noble Savage poems; he's a therapist.

KLS: [*Laughing*] Right, right.

LH: By looking back at my early work, I can see my own progress as a writer, and yet those early poems that have Noble Savage as therapist are not so different as the Savage Indian in *Savage Conversations*. He's the inquisitor for Mary Todd Lincoln. He asks, "Why did you do it?" And he forces her to confess that she has probably killed her kids with opiates that she was addicted to. "Why did I do it?" she asks herself in the play.

[*Pause*]

KLS: It's such a shocking revelation. And an incredibly powerful play. I see it as part of a long arc in your work of upending mainstream notions of American history and centering Indigenous voices. Thank you, LeAnne. I have enjoyed our time in New York very much.

LH: My pleasure, Kirstin. Thank you.

Notes

1. During the process of revising this interview, LeAnne Howe suggested the title as a reference to her short story "An American in New York," published in the 1989 collection, *Spider Woman's Granddaughters: Traditional Tales and Contemporary Writing by Native American Women*, edited by Paula Gunn Allen. Howe credits this short story as starting her literary career. *Spider Woman's Granddaughters* was reviewed in the *New*

York Times by award-winning novelist Ursula K. Le Guin, who highlighted Howe's story, focusing on its satirical critique of colonialism. In an editing note to Squint regarding the title choice, Howe said, "I'm only suggesting that in this interview, thirty years later, we're coming full circle. You and I. And giving homage to my 'coming out' as a writer." [All notes with this interview, as well as all editorial interpolations (ellipses and bracketed insertions) within the interview, are by the editor, who was also the interviewer.]

2. Howe shared this information after the interview: "People with schizophrenia are responsible for a disproportionate number of homicides; while they account for about 0.5 percent of the world's population, they are estimated to commit 6.5 percent of homicides worldwide, according to Dr. Olav Nielssen of the University of Sydney in Australia, the lead researcher on the new study released in 2009."

3. While revising this interview in the summer of 2020, LeAnne Howe added this comment regarding the interpretation of Choctaw concepts and language: "In fact, you can see that same process at work in our discourse just this past month. So many news outlets have spoken with us (Padraig [Kirwan] and I) about the Choctaw gift exchange between the Choctaws and the Irish. We've both been interviewed by many reporters. If you google *Famine Pots: The Choctaw-Irish Gift Exchange, 1847–Present*, or Padraig Kirwan, or me, or VOX, or Choctaws, Navajo, and Irish, etc., you can see that our chief used the word *iyyikowa*, which means selflessly serving those in need, for giving. This word isn't used by regular folks such as myself. Or other Choctaw friends that I talked to about it. We tend to use *ima*. Give. A verb. Chief is speaking on behalf of all of us. Three centuries later he is using diplomatic language that is elevated."

4. The Harvard Indians were five seventeenth-century Indians who attended Harvard Indian College, where tuition and housing were provided at no expense in expectation that the graduates would return as Christian missionaries to their home communities.

5. Susan Power is Dakota, an enrolled member of the Standing Rock Sioux tribe, and author of the award-winning novel *The Grass Dancer*.

6. LeAnne Howe, "Noble Savage Learns to Tweet," May 17, 2015, *Moving Poems: The Best Poetry Videos on the Web*, http://movingpoems.com/2015/05/noble-savage-learns -to-tweet-by-leanne-howe/.

Episode #3: LeAnne Howe

CAConrad / 2019

From *Occult Poetry Radio*, December 9, 2019. Printed by permission of CAConrad, *Occult Poetry Radio*. The interview has been edited for content for this volume. Editorial interpolations (bracketed content insertions and ellipses indicating omitted text) are by the volume editor.

Welcome to *Occult Poetry Radio*, where I interview poets about their occult practices and beliefs, as well as other paranormal activities they have experienced. Today is December 9, 2019, and I am your host, CAConrad. Today's episode is an interview with the poet LeAnne Howe. We talk about her extraordinary new book, *Savage Conversations*, her Native American heritage, and her firsthand accounts of interactions with ghosts and spirits, which are unlike anything I have ever heard. We also discuss her work in progress, which is a large book of poems based on eighteen ancient sacred mound sites she visited across North America. LeAnne Howe, born and raised in Oklahoma, is an enrolled citizen of the Choctaw Nation. Some awards include the Western Literature Association's 2015 Distinguished Achievement Award for her body of work; the inaugural 2014 MLA Prize for Studies in Native American Literatures, Cultures, and Languages; 2012 United States Artists Ford Fellowship; and a 2010 Fulbright Scholarship to Jordan. She received an American Book Award in 2002 for her first novel, *Shell Shaker*. Her most recent book, *Savage Conversations* (Coffee House Press, 2019), is the story of Mary Todd Lincoln and a Savage Indian spirit that Lincoln imagined was torturing her nightly, based on Mary Todd Lincoln's letters and reports from her doctors. Scholar Philip J. Deloria writes, "The book explodes with the stench and guilt and insanity that undergirds the American story." LeAnne is producing a new documentary, *Searching for Sequoyah*, with Ojibwe filmmaker James M. Fortier. The film is based in the US and Mexico where Sequoyah traveled while he was writing his Cherokee syllabary in 1841. The film will air in 2021 on public television. She is the Eidson Distinguished Professor in American Literature at the University of Georgia. We begin our conversation on the topic of spiritual tourism.

CAConrad: My spiritual heritage and my people are from Denmark and Ireland, and I keep that in mind when I'm practicing my magic that comes from my grandmothers and when I meet other white people who are what I call spiritual tourists, especially when it involves Native Americans in the United States. I try to gently talk to them about how maybe they need to investigate their own roots, but I wonder if maybe you have ever experienced this or what you might have to say about this.

LeAnne Howe: All the time!

[*Both laugh*]

LH: I can say that, throughout my life, . . . when people find out that I'm Native, they assume that, you know, that I have a sweat lodge in the back yard and I'm out there communing with nature or whatever, and that's not true either. But I have met dozens and dozens of people who also are exactly what you said, spiritual tourists, and it's awkward at times. I'll give you an example. I was in Iowa at a book reading and a woman heard that I was Native, and like "oh, there's someone who's Native in the back of the room." She came up, and she said, "Oh, you're Native American, you must have so much powerful medicine." And she grabbed me and pulled me to her, and I didn't know her, I had never seen her before, and I was pushing her away, like "Don't do that." She was offended because I rebuffed her. I think now: who walks up to another person and grabs them like "Oh sister," and not know me from Adam? But because she assumed that I had some kind of special medicine or something, she just grabbed me. So I learned a lesson. That's been a long time ago, but I've learned people look at us Natives in a certain way, and what I do these days is I kind of try to keep a low profile. I don't talk about being Native. Even though that's what I write about, even though that may or may not be the case, I think at some point it becomes unhealthy. I also think there are spiritual vampires, and they are there to suck the energy out of your body. For some people, [it] may be they are doing it unintentionally, but that is something I have tried to put up boundaries for—because it's unhealthy. As you have just said, most people come from these amazing heritages, Irish or German or English, [and] they all have spiritual practices that are not founded in the Judeo-Christian traditions. Find out what they are. Find your own heritage because it's fascinating, and as I said, it's not just ghosts are everywhere, but your own ancestors are waiting to explore that with you. That's my belief.

CAC: Could you please tell us about writing your book *Savage Conversations*?

LH: I started writing the book when I [was in] the Abraham Lincoln Library in Springfield, Illinois, where Lincoln's papers are, and many of the effects of the administration are there. In the library was a book *The Insanity File: The Case of Mary Todd Lincoln,* [first published in] 1986. Included was the trial of Mary Todd Lincoln, and in it she says an Indian came into her room every night and cut her up. And he cut her eyelids open, he scalped her, he cut a bone out of her cheek, and this is, you know, this cutting, that's torture. Yet at dawn's light—this is her word—he put everything back. Each night while she is in her room, an Indian is there to cut her up. This testimony is why she went into the asylum, and Robert Todd Lincoln takes her to trial to have her committed to Bellevue Place Sanitarium, where my book is set. Each night she tells people that she's being cut up. Now, all of that is one thing, but the fact that she blamed an American Indian for her insanity just set my soul on fire. I thought of all the things that Lincoln had done. He had hanged the thirty-eight Dakota who were, as far as he knew, innocent. He didn't know who the Indians were, what particular Indians had committed crimes; he just had them hanged. He sent the cavalry out west to exterminate American Indians. I thought of all the things Mary and her husband have done to harm Indians, and then for Mary to blame an American Indian for her mental state was just too much. I think my anger and my curiosity about her really are the basis of the book.

CAC: One of the voices in this new book is a noose that was used to hang Native Americans. You have an extraordinary story about interacting with this noose. Could you please tell us about this?

LH: When I started writing, I really wasn't concentrating on anyone but Mary Todd Lincoln and the Savage Indian. She had testified, "This is the person that cuts me up." I had written probably three-quarters of the book, and I was in Las Vegas, . . . about to take a shower. The lighting in the bathroom was very, very white. You know how those [hotel] bathrooms are; they are just very white and sterile-looking. I was just about to step into the shower when into the room floated right toward me a hangman's noose. And it just, it had a quiver to it, and it came right up, very close to my face, and it was very large. It was a hangman's noose, and I thought, "Oh, my god. This has got to be a sign, and this noose is going to begin talking." Sure enough, it did, and so . . . it's one of the three characters that are in *Savage Conversations.* I found out later that one noose had been found in 2014, and this kind of made me cry because I had written a lot of the conversation that the noose interjects between Mary Todd Lincoln and the Savage Indian, and when I found that out that one single noose was left from that 1862 hanging of the thirty-eight Dakotas, I cried a little thinking this must be part of the story because this noose wants to tell part of the story; therefore, it's voice is in the book. We can all say it was serendipity, or we can say it was coincidence. I don't believe that for a second. I believe that it wanted to tell the story, and so I had to follow it. That's what writers do. This is a sad story, you know? It's a sad, sad piece of American history, and I shed a lot of tears as I was writing this book.

CAC: Do you mind me asking you a little bit more about the noose?

LH: Oh, absolutely, I am happy to talk about "him"—because I didn't get a female energy from this noose. It was very male and robust, and also it's an instrument of death, so please, yeah, I'm happy to talk about it.

CAC: When you first saw the noose, you were in the bathroom, and you saw it in the reflection of the mirror or just coming right at you?

LH: It just came right at me. It just floated right at me, and then there we were, the two of us. I know it was a spirit. I know that, but nevertheless, it was right there, and there was something really otherworldly, of course, about the fact that this rope is a hangman's noose; it's in the rope. And what that sadness that happened in December in 1862 and what that rope represented—it was just, it was just really, I can't tell you how upsetting it was, but at the same time I thought, "Yeah, I have to tell this story." This instrument of death wants me to tell the story because my feeling about that history is maybe they hanged the right people, maybe they didn't, but they weren't given a trial, no one spoke to them, they didn't speak English, and I just felt like this rope knew that it had been used unjustly, and that's the story it tells, you know. So it became an integral part of the book. Who can say now what Lincoln was trying to do? Make the people in Minnesota feel better? But the people at that time were withholding food from the Natives. They were really the agents of death on the Dakota people, so it's just a tragic part of our history, and the fact that Mary Todd Lincoln said that she was being tortured and cut up—by an Indian spirit—I mean who talks like that? Maybe it's true, maybe she was, maybe indeed. I decided to believe her, and that's also part of this book. She said it, she testified in court, so why shouldn't we believe her? And if you have a strong sense of the power of spirits, then indeed we could say, "All right, Mary, you were being tortured, but there's a reason why," you know?

CAC: Wow. In 2014 when the noose was discovered, there were Native elders who went to put it to rest. Can you talk about that?

LH: The feeling was—and I spoke to one of the Dakota women who went to put this noose to sleep—to give it, give *it* peace. You know mostly in Native cultures, and I don't want to generalize, but at the same time I have to say this. Most Native cultures have animate and inanimate objects, and therefore, the rope was always animate. You know, it was made, it was fashioned, and once it was made, as in created, it became animate. And it had a history, it had a memory of what had happened, and so that animate rope with the memory of what happened wanted to be known. When they found it in the basement of Fort Snelling, then they brought in Dakota elders to put it to sleep, to rest. Peace. It wasn't you *need* to rest. Your energy *must* rest, and that's what they did.

[Howe reads a passage from page 81 of *Savage Conversations*.]

THE ROPE SEETHES,
REMEMBERING THE DAKOTA 38

September 1875, Batavia, Illinois

THE ROPE

First symptoms:
Flashes of light,
A hissing in the ears, like a locomotive
Rounding a tight curve,
A violent struggle, faces distorting,
Eyes bursting livid as the roots of tongues
Glottal stop the larynges.

They will *never* sing again.

Earth's gravity labors on,

Kick,
Kick,
Kick,
Kick,

I am not a judge.

CAC: Thank you so much. You've talked about seeing ghosts, and your family has as well. Can you tell us more about the ghosts and how they've maybe influenced your poetry?

LH: Well, I grew up with Native people, of course, and ghosts are part of our life. They're like, you know, there's like water, ghosts, they're elements. They're always, always around. I grew up in Oklahoma, and my great-grandmother was born around 1879, so my grandmother was born in 1899. What I'm suggesting is that it was just an average occurrence that there were ghosts in the house, there were ghosts outside, and my grandmother said, "You know we are not afraid of ghosts. They're here to tell us something, and if we sense that there is something bad, then we have medicines to keep them out of the house." So, for instance, we were driving, and I was with my grandfather and grandmother, and we were coming up on an old dirt road outside of Ada, and it's night. We had come from I think my great uncle's house at the time—I'm probably five or six—and we're driving, driving, and I'm standing up in the back seat of their old car and up ahead clear as day, we can see Indians. One woman had a red blanket around her, and others were with her, not quite as clear to me, but we could see her. My grandfather drove closer and closer and slowed down, thinking they were standing in the road, and *whoosh* they disappeared. My grandmother said, "It's okay. You know, they wanted us to know they're here, and that's a good thing." And we went on home. We never spoke about it again. Why? Because that was just the way things are. One time, Granny was sitting on the couch, and she smoked, and I woke up for some reason—I was staying with her at the time—and she's sitting there in the dark. I got up, and she said, "Old Lum Jones just went up through the trees. He died." I said, "He died?" She said, "Yes, he died, and I saw him go up through the trees," and sure enough the next day the next-door neighbor was dead. So. That was just the way things were. You know, sometimes I thought, "She's scary, she's really scary," but she taught me especially—I think I was her favorite—not to be afraid. I'm not afraid of ghosts and spirits. In fact, they're another element just like water, and they are here usually to teach us something, but you can occasionally run up on someone who is really bad. I'll tell you another story, and then I will stop.

CAC: Oh, no, please don't stop!

LH: When I met my husband, he took me back to Iowa, and he was driving me around places at night that were across the dam in Iowa City and various places, and he said, "This is an old park where we use to go picnicking." And in the distance there was an image of this horrific spirit, and I could see it clearly. Besides this yellow-looking garment it had on, this entity had a mouth that was red and like it had eaten something, and it was dripping blood. I could see it in the distance, and I hollered, "Stop the car, stop the car, stop the car, get away! We have to get—" He was totally unprepared, and I said, "Stop, stop. If you don't stop, I am going to run the other way." That ghost, that entity, that angry evil thing was in the distance. And we backed out all the way out of the park, and we drove the other way, and I said, "We have to get across the water, we have to get across the dam." Because they mostly—in the belief system I was raised with—can't cross water to get you. . . . I know how crazy I sound, but that's an example of something that is threatening, and when you see that bad entity, you have to go the other way, and you have to protect yourself. So [for us] Natives, you know there's all kinds of reasons we carry certain things with us. For protection, to remind us of the love our family has given us, but that's just an example of something bad that had happened there. And here's the caveat. Later, Jim said, "Oh, I forgot that there was a big party that happened there" before his high school years, "and someone had run over a girl in a tent and killed her in the night. The driver of the car that night was drunk." I said, "You took me to this place where this horrific event happened?" I don't know if it was the one that was killed. She was in a tent, and someone drove over her body. I don't know that. But I know that that site holds bad things, and I also know that even if I were to go back to Iowa, I can't go back to that site.

CAC: You say that ghosts are an element. I don't think I've ever heard anybody say that before. That's amazing. By the way, you said, "I know I sound crazy." I think, you know, all of us are going to sound crazy on this program, so it doesn't matter. That's my aim.

[*Both laugh*]

CAC: So you actually give voice to the ghost in this new book, *Savage Conversations*, the noose. Are there any other ghosts whom you have given voice to?

LH: Well, yes, and there are animals that I've given voice to. Big Mother Porcupine is a person that appeared in *Shell Shaker*, and she comes in the form of a porcupine, and then she also comes in as a spirit. . . . My characters go out to visit her in the woods, around McAlester. And she also is the one that gives the medicine to help the two people in the book to succeed with what they are about to do. Big Mother Porcupine is the one that tells them how to prevent this really evil spirit from taking away this other character. So, yeah, I've written about other ghosts and spirits. In *Miko Kings*, my second novel, there was a baseball team, a whole baseball team, that one of my characters [sees], because Indians invented baseball, and it was [called] "base and ball." You know, it's got four quadrants, you run counterclockwise like a tornado, it's a game without time, hello! Indians don't have the clock and the bell. In that book there are spirits as well that come into the house to tell the story about what happened to Miko Kings. It's just a fact of life. I am pretty sure if we just open and remain open, there are spirits all around us, and some are good, some are bad. Not everyone in the neighborhood is great, so it's a good thing to have this awareness, and the knowing has served me well in my lifetime. It's part of my art as well. That's kind of the best of all relations is that we know they are there, and we want to be open to messages. I bet everybody you know hears the messages or sees the spirits, and a lot of times people just don't want to admit it, or they have to wait until they've known you for many, many years [to tell you]. Well, many American Indians are kind of not like that; [instead, they'll say,] "Well, here's what happened last week."

CAC: You've said that your grandmother helped you be open to these things. Do you believe that the noose knew that, and were you frightened at all when that first happened?

LH: I was terrified! Here I am writing about the thirty-eight Dakota that Abraham Lincoln hanged in 1862, and yet, when the noose floated through the wall, so to speak, into that bathroom, and I'm standing there thinking, "Oh my God," and it floated right up within twelve inches of my face, and it's seething mad, but it also has a story to tell, I was frightened, no question about it. Then I thought, "It's trying to tell me something, so I have to deal with it." Deal with my own fear and then be open to what it is, and from then on out, I heard what it was saying, and then the noose became kind of a joker, in the "savage conversation." He breaks the fear because it's a heavy little story. You know Mary Todd Lincoln was really a force to be reckoned with. He is the one who breaks the spell, tells the story, the really harsh story: "Yes, America hanged these thirty-eight Indians." The rope knew what they said as they were standing on the scaffolding in Mankato, Minnesota, and so the rope then becomes this truth teller and carries the energy. Mary Todd Lincoln in *Savage Conversations* is talking more about what she wanted and how she supported the hanging of the thirty-eight and how she hated American Indians, and so the story is rounded out. That vision and that entity told why Mary said an American Indian was cutting her up at night. This is what is in the poem "Savage Indian Laments." It's from the book *Savage Conversations.*

[Howe reads from pages 28–30, *Savage Conversations*.]

SAVAGE INDIAN LAMENTS

July 4, 1875
Bellevue Place Sanitarium, 333 S. Jefferson Street
Batavia, Illinois

Savage Indian walks amid all the clutter in her sitting room. Mary Todd Lincoln paces.

SAVAGE INDIAN
I know isolation.
Silence.
The slow descent downward,
Lost somewhere in midair.

Gar Woman, I have crippling doubt, but
I surrender nothing, not even in death.

He looks at their surroundings.

I no longer have to worry.
That doesn't mean I am not suspicious of the living.
They enter my dreams uninvited.

In Dakhóta land, they are pulling down the last of our dead,
Bodies of men and women hanged by a rope of lies.

When I was a human being,
I would sing the air thick with Dakhóta songs.

December 26, 1862.
In one hundred and fifty years, the citizens of Mankato
will shiver,
Asking why their ancestors hanged thirty-eight Dakhóta
Indians over a handful of hens' eggs.

When I look at your world, I weep
Because in the end, even your life is a captivity account.
Maybe we are all captives of one sort or the other.

He stops and drinks water from her china tea cup.

For the thirty-eight lives abandoned.

In that moment in Mankato, I was misplaced.
Maybe the Nightjars carried my spirit to safety,
Back to the beginning, even before Mother Earth existed.
You are probably wondering when. What millennium?
Because in your eyes every hour is measured.

To die alone while dying with thirty-seven others.

This is where I tell you about my friend's dying.
A death song, he sang it, then we sang together.
On the platform in Mankato, we tried to grasp hands,
shouting to the winds,
Mni Sóta Maḳoce, land where the waters reflect the skies,
The land where we die.
Words caught in our throats. Choked by a muscular rope.

Savage Indian raises the tea cup again to salute The Rope.

Rope, he held fast.

The Rope takes a bow.

Eighteen sixty-two, almost like a birthday.
Tiny needles sew shut the muslin cloth around our faces.
Buried in a mass grave only to be dug up,
Stolen by physicians to be used as medical cadavers,
Later stored in cast-iron pots.

Still,
Our bodies cramped and squirmed in the wind, our
spirits scattered.
All of us, Gar Woman, still hang
And you dressed in a stinking nightshift,
The one you refuse to remove all these months,
Can never cover the past.

The soldiers are pulling on their boots,
They are not the ones they think they are.

When I am myself as I am tonight, every word is a weapon.
When I am myself as I am tonight, why can't I forget what
happened and
Take you amid the dried-up tingling in my head,
The dried-up prickle between my legs,
The ragged filaments of desire.

Oh, I lied to settlers, I lied to preachers,
But Gar Woman, you are not who you claim to be,
You bring a child into the world and intensely regret it,
Despite your theatrical tears for pity when another son dies.

You believe you know what must be done with your
Brews and tainted teas.

But I have seen the ghosts of Abraham, Eddie, Willie,
even Tad,
Shrink when you enter a room,
Shadows escaping your burning sun.

What happens next, Gar Woman?
You've swallowed all but one of your eggs.

Savage Indian grabs Mary Todd Lincoln by her shoulders
and pulls her to him.

Because the wind refuses your touch
Because the insects abandon the ground where you sleep
Because your hair wilts the prairie grasses
Because at dawn every breath is a trial
Because with your eyes sewn open you still see nothing
Because everything you touch leaves a bruise.

The muskets are being reloaded
The carbines are being reloaded
The large-bore rifles are being reloaded
The Gatling guns are being reloaded.
Emancipate me!

Fire!

CAC: That was amazing.

LH: Thank you. Well, I think, you know, the kind of narrative that the rope has in *Savage Conversations*: he's the ice breaker. He's also useful as a foil. I think that kind of energy that he embodies in the book is really, for me, part of my southern writer identity. I know I'm not from the Deep South, but our tribe is, and so we kind of have this way of breaking the spell, breaking the ice through irony, through a bit of comedy, through comic relief, and it helps. Because with our history, frankly we could either cry all the time, or we can break that spell. And that's how I see these spirits in most of my work. The spirits come to break the spell; they break the heaviness of what's happened to the five big tribes, what's happened through removal, what's happened through the way in which the federal government has abused us, historically speaking. There is a reason there are no Natives left in Georgia. They were all pushed out. We can either cry about that or we can find a way to write that narrative with us in it. That's how I see my job, as kind of a foil against desperation.

CAC: You're also working on a new book now about mounds. Could you please talk about these poems?

LH: My new poetry is called *The Book of Mounds*. I also do a lot of field work—I think every poet does—and I visited about eighteen mound complexes in Canada and the US, throughout Native North America. I'm writing about the entities that are the mounds themselves. For instance, the Choctaw—I'm Choctaw—our mother mound is in Winston County, Mississippi. The Choctaws have a giant platform mound, but these are sites of powerful energy. Visiting these sites really taught me about the different kinds of energy because, like human beings or like anything else animate, not all mound sites are good. They're not. They can be powerful for various reasons—their purposes are known unto them because they are alive, just like we are. I have been at a mound site that was full of anger, and it's in Oklahoma. My colleague Monique Mojica and I were writing a play called *Sideshow Freaks and Circus Injuns*, and we were visiting a mound site in Oklahoma that was deadly. When we approached it—we always approach these mounds with a certain humility, we always bring some kind of gift that we can leave at the site, being tobacco or another remedy—we got completely hoodwinked and had to exit that site because there was such a powerful energy that did not want us to be there. I was concerned because I felt the energy follow us as we were driving away in the car. It was really a very troubling moment. That site is, I don't know, probably, oh a couple of thousand years old. So [now] that site is off limits to me. It's like this place that we were at in Iowa. I can't go back; I can't. I can read signs. On the other hand, we were visiting the Snake Mound in Peterborough up in Canada, Ontario, which was a wonderfully warm and powerful experience. The snake is pointing toward the United States, at another serpent mound in Ohio. You could feel the energy source moving back and forth, and we were with a lot of—

CAC: Back and forth between the two mounds?

LH: We didn't know what the other energy source was, but you could feel this. It was very powerful. When we got back to Ohio, to the serpent mound, what one of the medicine people told us is those two mounds are in conversation, so you have to be very respectful. It may look like it's a long distance, but spirit way it's not all that far away. It's just right there. The people who built these mounds, sometimes two, three, four thousand years ago, knew the power that was part of that dynamic. So we wrote the play *Sideshow Freaks and Circus Injuns*, which engaged these mounds. Then I'm writing a separate book called *The Book of Mounds* and also working with another scholar, a literary scholar, Chadwick Allen, and we want to bring a lot of voices of people who worked on these projects. We had a four-year grant from SSHRC [Social Sciences and Humanities Research Council] to look at mounds and mound culture. [Chadwick and I are] doing an academic book, and I have the poetry, and then Monique and I wrote this play that we performed, not formally, but we've rehearsed it and performed in summer of 2017. I've done a lot of work thinking about the power and the energy that Indigenous people brought to building those sites and the power used for ceremonies. Typically, many of these sites are high up, and they can reenergize people who are open. So don't be weary, but go with a good heart when you visit these mound sites all over North America. See for yourselves, and you can feel what these powerful people worked with the higher energy sources around us and what it created. We still have them today. I think it's pretty amazing. The oldest mound site is in Louisiana in North America, and it's something like seven thousand years old. Amazing.

CAC: Have you visited that one?

LH: Yes, I have. Yeah, yeah, of course. That's at Poverty Point, and I've written a lot about Poverty Point because there is a giant red-tailed hawk, the body of a female hawk, and it's pointing west. Her beak has been dug up because they thought she had gold in her beak. She's facing west, and her head is turned like this [*Howe demonstrates*], and her wings are just so, as if she's landing. It's this huge mound site. I think that these kinds of knowledges can help us heal today. We're in a very chaotic period of time, centering ourselves, going to a mound site and praying; and going with a good heart will help us to recover from this chaos. That's my message.

CAC: Could you please tell us about the experience you and Monique had at one of the mounds?

LH: Monique Mojica and me and Ric Knowles and many more actors and scholars were all working on this project—

CAC: Is he the archeologist?

LH: No, Ric Knowles is a theater scholar. An archeologist met us at the site, but he wasn't part of the program. We were there as part of the SSHRC grant. Ric Knowles had written the grant [proposal]. Over the course of four years, we visited eighteen mound sites. Monique Mojica lives in Toronto, and [our] *Sideshow Freaks and Circus Injuns* was a result of all of the mounds we visited, and again there's an element of breaking the spell with humor in the play. We were working with American Indian Studies scholar Chadwick Allen. At that time, he was a professor at Ohio State University; he's now at the University of Washington. There is a mound site in Ohio we went to visit, and the interesting thing about this site is that it's almost all gone. They have plowed and plowed and plowed, trying to get rid of this mound site, but it's still got its footprint, and you can see it when you pull up to the site. So we're there, and we're walking around the site, and Monique and I caught this sound in the wind. We can hear it, and so we go to ground, first one of us, then both. We crouched together, and we could still hear this very high-pitched singing, so we began to sing along with this sound, and Monique recorded our singing on her smartphone. Our colleague Chadwick Allen could see and feel the power that was coming down from the sky or in the atmosphere, and it was a little girl singing, and we were singing with her. The park ranger who had given us access to the site and shown us around was, I think, unsettled and perhaps afraid. He acted disturbed and fearful anyway, and he just started talking and talking and talking, and Chad is trying to get him to back up, saying in effect, "Will you please be quiet because this little girl has come to sing, this site is hers." [The experience becomes] one of the poems I'll write in my collection *The Book of Mounds*. It was so powerful, and her little voice was so strong, and she was with us trying to say, "I'm here, I'm here, always here." And this western-trained park ranger, bless his heart, just couldn't stop talking because his worldview was shaken, and he was afraid.

CAC: Could you please read from the mound project for us?

LH: Oh, I'd be happy to! This is the twins. In a lot of Native cosmology, there are always twins. Well, that's kind of consistent around the world too.

CAC: Gemini.

LH: Yes, absolutely, and so it's also true of the cosmic world. This is part of the opening of the play that Monique and I wrote. I'm going to chant this, and normally this would be performed by the twins that would walk on stage and chant. While I'm chanting, visualize twins that represent the two energies. They would walk on the stage and open the performance:

[*Chants in Choctaw*]
The songchants repeat four times on the stage.
"Because you are holding on to me, I am not dead yet."
[*Chants in Choctaw*]

Falcon Man: First two Choctaw hunters are crying by the Alibamu river before the age of corn. They hear a call and response song coming from a mound near the river. The two Choctaw men see her. She appears reflected in the moonlight. She brings a gift and instructions. Her name is Ohoyo Chishba Osh, the Unknown Woman, Corn Woman. I become irresistible in a dress made of (*speaks Choctaw*) brilliant white stars, serene yet steamy. I use the light coming from inside me to attract attention. Falcon Man, what they will say is her poem is (*speaks Choctaw*) the power of thought represented as food.

CAC: Thank you!

LH: Thank you for asking about this project. It's been a while, since 2017, when Monique and I read this, and we had so many spiritual events happen to us, and so many cosmic experiences in the four years that we took to visit these eighteen mound sites. It taught me to come to these sites, to come to these mounds, as people with an open heart and with a sense of purpose. I'm hoping to be able to bring Monique to UGA in the 2020–2021 academic year.

CAC: Do you mind if we talk about the anthology [*When the Light of the World Was Subdued, Our Songs Came Through: A Norton Anthology of Native Nations Poetry*] at the end here? I really want everybody to know about this anthology coming out. When I was younger, I was a big fan of Jerome Rothenberg's anthology, *Technicians of the Sacred.*

LH: Yes.

CAC: And then he also did *Shaking the Pumpkin,* which was a Native American anthology—

LH: That's right. . . .

CAC: You have just completed this anthology. Can you talk about this anthology? It's very important.

LH: Yes, we are so delighted about it. Joy [Harjo] asked us to work on it. Joy Harjo, Jennifer Foerster, and I are probably the—I don't know what to call us—the mothers of the manuscript, in that we helped shaped the body of the manuscript by working with other Native poets throughout Native North America. We have, I believe, five regions in the anthology, and within those regions, there were sometimes eight or four or seven poets working on the regions, depending on who could work at that time. Native poets within the regions also brought poems into the anthology. The earliest poem is [from] 1678 by a Native author we don't know much about other than he wrote "Elegy" and his name was Eleazar. He was one of the Harvard Indians.[1] We open with that [northeast] region of the country and go south and then continue to go around Native North America beginning with the oldest works and move forward in each region. Our youngest poet in the anthology was born in 1983. It spans Native Nations in the United States, [including] Hawaii and Alaska. It's a beautiful collection. Norton is the publisher. It'll be out in fall 2020. I am really proud to have been part of this collection, and we worked very hard to have poets from all these regions. It's an amazing volume. . . . I'm so proud of the work. It's kind of amazing.

CAC: It is. It's so amazing, and it's great that in 2019 we have [Joy Harjo as] the first Native American poet laureate of the United States.

LH: I know! [*Howe claps.*] Yes, Joy, we are all so proud of you! It's just the most exciting time. I got to go to her inaugural reading in Washington, DC. That was so amazing! Natives from all over the United States and non-Natives were there to celebrate this important event. I am so happy. . . .

CAC: And this is the first time that Norton has published an anthology of Native poetry, correct?

LH: That's correct. . . .

CAC: Thank you so much for taking the time to have his interview with me for *Occult Poetry Radio*. I am excited for this anthology and your new book on mounds coming out.

LH: CA, thank you for having me. You are an amazing poet, and I am the one who is honored to be on your program. I feel we are relatives.

CAC: Thank you. Much love to you.

LH: Much love to you.

[Musical interlude]

CAC: I am looking forward to her new book of poems on the mounds. That is all we have for you today, and I hope you buy LeAnne Howe's new book, *Savage Conversations*. Please find our link to her website for more information on the upcoming documentary and anthology. I am your host, CAConrad, and please come back for future episodes of *Occult Poetry Radio*.

[Theme music plays.]

Note

1. See endnote 4 in "'An American in New York': LeAnne Howe" in this volume for information on the Harvard Indians.—Ed.

Genre-Sliding on Stage with Playwright LeAnne Howe

Jen Shook / 2020

Previously unpublished interview conducted January 3, 2020. Printed by permission of Jen Shook, Visiting Fellow, Penn State Center for Humanities & Information.

Jen Shook's interview with LeAnne Howe took place on January 3, 2020, via the videoconferencing platform Zoom and was solicited by Kirstin L. Squint for *Conversations with LeAnne Howe.* Shook is an expert in Indigenous women's drama and an experienced director and dramaturge. Howe's work as playwright has garnered less critical attention than her fiction and theoretical writing; however, that may change, given the reviews of her 2019 play in verse, *Savage Conversations.* Howe and Shook discuss the play and much more.

Jen Shook: I'm excited to get to talk with you. I want to focus primarily on theater and performance, but of course that will interweave with other things. We will talk about the pros and cons of thinking about genre. But I wanted to start out by asking how you would describe yourself in relation to theater and performance?

LeAnne Howe: You know, I don't know that I think of myself first as a performance artist, although that's where I started, as a performer. When I was working with Roxy Gordon in the 1980s, we probably performed every week in the Dallas-Fort Worth Metroplex and around Texas. That's really how I began my career as a performer. I mean, we performed in so many locations; there was a place called Caravan of Dreams that was built by the Bass Brothers in the eighties, and people like William S. Burroughs came there. I think we opened one night for Burroughs, and there are many other examples. Roxy Gordon was of Choctaw descent, but he also was a coauthor on several of the plays that we wrote and performed. We did those almost as rehearsals for all these readings around Texas, so at that time we read everywhere, and as the performance grew, the bodies of our plays grew as well. That's how I began, writing with him and performing. Then we were involved with a whole group of people across D-FW. We read with Tim Seibels—who else, poet Robert Trammel, poet Jennifer Kidney, the Black Hat Poet, a lot of people who were well-known poets and writers at the time, and people from abroad. That began the work of *Indian Radio Days*. *Big PowWow* was first; then we had kind of a repertoire of back and forth between us with the band, and Roxy then developed a bigger band and a bigger, broader show for himself and his readings. And he created all these CDs. That went on probably from 1983 to 1989, so I was rehearsing in performance and learning how to draw in an audience with my prose. I just turned in my early work from this era as part of my archive at the University of Oklahoma, and I probably have that many [*holds up hand to show about two inches*] posters of work that Roxy and I did. Big posters, small posters, that's gone into the archive. Some of them I had completely forgotten about. For instance, we opened once for Paula Gunn Allen, who was coming through D-FW. I think she read at Thistle Hill in Fort Worth. At the time they would host readings for local writers in the Fort Worth area. And then we always had these big blowout parties. We would get a group together and stage some of the plays. Our own, or somebody else's. That is how I thought of myself for the longest time, a performance artist, and then I branched out to short fiction. I'd always, always, always written poems early on in the seventies, but I never thought of myself as a poet, and I still have trouble thinking of myself as a poet or even a performer. I would say that I am a writer, and that's how I think of myself, just a writer who slides between genres and often performs on stage. I credit the theatrical work that we did for pushing me to become a fiction writer. For instance, in *Big PowWow*, there's a character, the Old Ghost, who is a Choctaw bone picker. The research I did at that time in Texas and in Mississippi, looking at our bone picking traditions and who those old bone pickers were, went into the plays and later my fiction. At first, I interviewed my mother to talk about bone picking, and this is a long time before she died. She said, "Oh, I don't know anything about that," and then later after she became really sick, she said, "I do know that, I do." There were these old ladies who were bone pickers when she was a little girl. They were Choctaw bone pickers who would go down into the cemetery and pick the bones of the dead. That became part of a staged performance of bone picking in the play *Big PowWow*, and it grew and grew until it became a character in my novel *Shell Shaker*. Then before that there was another play that we did. All of that comes out of the seventies and eighties performance experience.

JS: What was the impulse that led you into doing that theatrical art to begin with?

LH: I know exactly how our collaborations began. It was a newspaper ad that Roxy Gordon put in a Dallas arts newspaper. He said, "I am looking for Choctaws to come together and work with and collaborate with. If you know any Choctaw artists out there, please contact me." So I just called him. . . . I may or may not have that newspaper clipping in my archive that I have now turned over to OU. That was the beginning of our collaboration.

JS: Wow.

LH: From that newspaper ad we just got together, and I went over to Roxy and Judy Gordon's house in Dallas because I was living in Fort Worth. We ended up doing automatic writing, and it was kind of shocking to both of us because we were not alike, our literary voices were very different, but they clicked for a performance piece.

JS: Interesting. And then how did WagonBurner Theatre Troop come about?

LH: WagonBurner began because I left Texas. I went to Iowa and met my husband at a conference in South Dakota, so I was really lonely for Natives, for American Indians to hang out with. I wanted to start a performance group. I wanted to perform *Indian Radio Days*, but I needed a whole group. At that time at the University of Iowa there were quite a few Indian students. This would have been 1989, 1990–1991, something like that. It took us about a year to coalesce, maybe a bit longer, and then we started Wagon-Burner Theatre Troop, and we started performing all over. There was a man, whom I have to say I didn't like, who got interested in us, and I ended up cursing him out on the phone, but he was producing newsletters, and so he did an interview with me. WagonBurner went on because we had a lot of graduate students who have now gone on to their own academic careers. We even performed at the Smithsonian as WagonBurner Theatre Troop.

JS: Oh, wow.

LH: Yeah, that was really a fun time, but you know people in theater groups argue all the time.

JS: Yes! [*Chuckles*]

LH: That just came with the territory. After about 1995 we broke up, but we've since come back together, stayed in touch.

JS: I think one of my introductions to learning about WagonBurner was seeing a photo of Jodi Byrd performing in one of the pieces and thinking— . . .

LH: That's right!

JS: So when I read Jodi Byrd writing about *haksuba*—

LH: [*Laughs*]

JS: And saying, "in LeAnne Howe's work, the generative chaos of cultural collision,"[1] I'm thinking, *innnteresting.* [*Laughs*]

LH: Oh, Jodi was hilarious! That girl can act, and she and another woman did this duo on stage—I have pictures of all that—and they were absolutely hilarious. Their timing was really good. She did a piece that she built into our play with Claudine Levi-Echofemme, and it was a scream. It was just so absolutely funny. Claire Cardwell would come on stage—she was tall, she is a very tall Cherokee woman—and she would come on stage as Claudine Levi-Echofemme and interrupt these two women—Jodi was one of them—who were on stage. And the three of them had these really funny scenes. It was vaudeville, you know, and it was just a lot of fun, and we have recordings from that. Those days, we recorded ourselves two or three times, so that was the life of *Indian Radio Days.* I've been told that the Wampanoags have regularly staged *Indian Radio Days* and have rewritten parts of it too. I said, "Yes, absolutely." Roxy and I wanted other tribes to mix this up, so it wouldn't be so southeastern-centric, and write your own jokes and your own comedy into the larger play. I have several of the posters that the Wampanoags did, and it was three or four years I think that they performed *Indian Radio Days.* We did the same thing at Vermillion, South Dakota. The Sioux did it, and I went to see the show. This was before Russell Means passed away. All these Native students in Vermillion parodied Russell Means, and he was in the audience. One of the girls came off stage and went down into the audience and said, "Oh, look at him!" The gag was she mistook him [Russell Means] for a white man in the audience. They brought him on stage and broke the fourth wall with this gag. I was watching in the audience, laughing, and I nearly fell out of my chair. It was so funny. Great memories, and the show had legs with Native performers; it's really been surprising to me. Roxy died in 2000, so he never got to see the show travel. He was quite ill and passed, I'm sorry to have to say. He was such a good writer, such a good and interesting performer and man. He is survived by his two sons. His wife, Judy, also worked with us on the shows. She did the costuming and all the artwork; it was a family affair. Those were great times. Thanks for asking about them.

JS: Absolutely. Well, funny that you mention that newsletter. I want to come back to the vaudeville angle, but I can't remember if I told you Ann Haugo[2] has the boxes of copies of that newsletter in her garage.

LH: Oh, my God!

JS: And she and I have been talking about trying to create some sort of response work with them. At first, we talked about digitizing them, and then we said, "It's clear before even asking that there is some debate in some of the newsletter issues that perhaps some people would not like to have digitized online." And then in talking with some people, we have learned a bit more about some of those debates. I don't know what you would like to say about that, if anything.

LH: The gentleman who did those newsletters is not a bad guy, but I was much more outspoken than I am today. I didn't like it that he had this very purist idea about what Native theater is and who Native people are. He looked at us and assumed things, including about me. He had an expectation of what Natives look like, what Natives say, what Natives write, and that was all trapped in his own stereotype. Now, he has since apologized to me for that kind of nonsense. But he just came to the show and just ripped us all a new one. He said it [our play] was disrespectful to Indian people. Every one of us in the cast were Native, different tribes. He said we were disrespectful, we used language, harsh language, and that we were making fun of our own people. I said, "What the fuck is the matter with you? Of course, we are!" You know. "You didn't grow up Indian, we did. You don't know what that means," and he didn't even like to hear the word "Indian." And I said, "My grandmother uses that word, I've grown up with that word, and you are not going to take it away from us." I just read him the riot act, and I was all over him. It still makes me mad. And he hated the show. He thought we had just gone too far at making fun of ourselves; it was disrespectful to Indian people. I said, "You aren't our policeman. You're this white guy from South Dakota!" In truth I don't know if he was from North or South Dakota.

JS: [*Laughs*]

LH: But that's what I told him. Later he might have thought about it or whatever, but he apologized for having the expectation of some kind of, I don't know, colonizer. "You don't look like an Indian." Well, you don't look like a white man! [*Laughs*] I don't know what that means either! That was how that began, and we did not see eye to eye, and I think he ended up publishing a respectful Q&A, but there's some "fuck" words in there.

[*Both laughing*]

LH: That's what I said, and I might have even said worse at the time, but that's how that came about. I was just reading William Yellow Robe's plays. He'll have a wonderful collection coming out from SUNY, his collected works. I don't know that I think there is yet a good definition of "Native Theater." "Oh, it's by an American Indian playwright. Oh, it's performed by—you know—insert Native performer's name." The point is that I think those core elements of being a "Native American play" are hard to pin down because for Natives it's hard to adhere to one kind of idea of redness. I think this kind of fluidity is unique to American Indian theater.

JS: Yeah, I've noticed, particularly within the boundaries of what we current call the United States, trying to describe Native and American Indian theater, there is often an assumption that "Oh, you're talking about the oral traditions and the ancient stories." I say, "No, I'm talking about plays that were written last year, being performed right now, they're brand new," and then people will say, "Oh, so you're talking about the nineteenth century." Then there were the efforts of playwrights like Hanay Geiogamah to come up with a critical vocabulary to talk about his Native theater in the 1970s, but that doesn't really work with the way that we are critically talking about sovereign specificity now.

LH: Right, right.

JS: Geiogamah's approach to ceremony and survivability—you know some pieces of that still resonate with contemporary writing, and some of them feel dated. You know they are thirty, forty, fifty years old at this point.

LH: I agree. I do think, because of land and specificity, young Native playwrights build homage of place into their work, but it isn't necessarily place-based. It's not there. And that's okay because things are changing, they have changed, and we have changed. I just got a card from my friend who has come out with a book called *"Help Indians Help Themselves": The Later Writing of Gertrude Simmons Bonnin (Zitkála-Šá)* edited by Jane Hafen. Bonnin is talking about performance, and she is talking about her performances in the latter part of her life. So it's the later work, but she is still performing, you know? We're nothing like her. Our work is not like hers, and yet I can see elements of Native theater in her work. But it's different, and it's also nineteenth century, and now we're talking about twenty-first-century Native theater. It's exciting to me that we are evolving, yes indeed, we go back to our land. But not in the way that is expected. I think that's the best I can do.

JS: One of the things that's been so interesting to me about the ways that I've encountered your plays and watched them circulate—and this has been true for Mary Kathryn Nagle's work certainly and several other contemporary playwrights—is that they are pieces that are very *portable*, for lack of a better word. [They can be staged] in museums or in bookstores or in community centers or in hallways. Or with or without a set, with or without costumes, with or without original design elements, and that makes them portable to YouTube and podcasts and audio recordings and conferences.

LH: Yes.

JS: Which is really necessary, probably, when the whitestream regional theater institutions have not been supporting Native playwrights.

LH: And still don't.

JS: Still don't, right? Are slowly getting on the bandwagon, but yeah, that kind of work also seems to really mesh well with that vaudeville sensibility. That's how vaudeville grew up, and it's also a kind of critical, parody, archival—I don't know quite what word I'm trying to say—but a way to incorporate stereotypes and comment on them at the same time. Like *The Mascot Opera*, which I'm a huge fan of. I love watching the way technology intersects and that you are absolutely the opposite of shying away from stereotypes and painful recirculated images, but instead use the remixed image in a really productive way, right?

LH: Yeah.

JS: I just stumbled across the video of Noble Savage on Twitter.[3]

LH: [*Laughs*] I love that!

JS: Which I had not seen until recently. How do you see those older forms like vaudeville and barn performance interacting with technology? Do they feed each other? Is that something you thought about with *Indian Radio Days*?

LH: No, you know those things come later, and the writing or the words come first, and then I think, "Eh, this would be good for x, y, and z. Or wouldn't it be funny to do x, y, and z?" There's this wonderful short video[4] that Heid Erdrich did—Louise Erdrich's sister—and Louise comes into focus in a costume and is holding up a mask, and Heid says about the making of the video, "Well, we had an idea, but it all just begins to work." I think that's typical for Native people: you've got an idea, and you have some language perhaps or not. And all of a sudden because of the humor you then end up staging these crazy things that are funny, as if we are only entertaining ourselves, then we *are* only entertaining ourselves, and that's the most important thing. I think that's exactly how art happens. So Heid was talking about this, and they had an idea they were gonna do this, and then, it just worked. I think Native people give themselves permission to play in ways that other artists who are very serious may not. I don't want to build more stereotypes necessarily, but I believe Natives have a different way of making art. [My poems] "Noble Savage Learns to Tweet" and "Noble Savage Sees a Therapist" came about because I thought they were funny. And, in my version of their story, Noble Savage and Indian Sports Mascot are lovers.

JS: Right!

LH: [*Laughs*] Of course, they are! And it just sort of happened. Then I ran into Heid, and she gave me the name of Jonathan Thunder, and I sent him my work. I asked him to do the animation for it, and *voila*! It just worked. I want to do a whole series of those where I build the characters together theatrically. The two start as vaudeville actors, and then they finish up as an old married couple, living inside the Museum of the American Indian, you know.

JS: [*Laughs*]

LH: That's where that story will go, one of these days, when I get ten minutes to do some other stuff that I've been wanting to do.

JS: That's great! I look forward to that very much.

LH: I think that would be really funny, and that's usually how I start all my projects. "Well, wouldn't it be funny . . ."

JS: . . . Once upon a time in Chicago, I ran a theater; I founded and directed a company called Caffeine Theatre. Our mission was to mine the poetic tradition to explore social questions. We were known as this fusion of poetry and performance in a way that, to me, made such absolute sense, not only because poetry and theater are related, but also because—

LH: They're sisters.

JS: Right, but also when you look back in multiple worldwide cultural traditions, Aristotle used the word "poetry" to talk about plays.

LH: Yes!

JS: So there I was teaching Aristotle at Columbia College Chicago, and people were confused that we were putting poetry and theater together.

LH: And that sounds so wild, doesn't it, considering their histories?

JS: Yes, and that is why I am very much attuned to how people describe those hybrid pieces like *Savage Conversations* where critics start to get obsessed with "Well, is it a poem, is it a play, is it a novel?" I found this description where the *LA Review of Books* calls it "a play/poem/novel/historical nightmare."[5]

LH: [*Laughs*]

JS: [The review is by] Nathan Scott McNamara.

LH: Okay, great.

JS: And then McNamara calls you a "genre chemist."

LH: Oh, I like it. That's nice!

JS: Isn't that nice? "Genre chemist"! "Mixing disparate textual, visual, and auditory techniques to create singular narrative energy."

LH: Wow!

JS: Isn't that great?

LH: Can you send me a copy, or send me the link to that?

JS: Absolutely, I will. Absolutely.

LH: A genre chemist. [*Chuckles*]

JS: A genre chemist, I know! And then I know that you talk about remix a little bit in *Mascot Opera*, and because of your references to Baz Luhrmann, of course, you can't talk about that without talking about remix. I was happy to see you use the word "remix" in a discussion, and then Annette Lapointe in the *New York Journal of Books* talking about *Savage Conversations* says, "It is a striking hybrid. A play in verse, never meant to be staged. A novel."[6] To which I thought, "Oh, yeah. That's what everybody said about all the plays that Caffeine Theatre did."

[*Both laughing*]

LH: Never meant to stage it? Mmm, not true!

JS: That's how people talk about Yeats and Lorca and Eliot. Then she goes on to say it's "a novel that resists prose structure." Which again, what does that mean? It's like looking for Native people to look a certain way. Looking for prose structure to look a certain way.

LH: Yeah, okay. She's dead wrong. I mean, I started this project to be performed.

JS: Well, I'm not surprised to hear that.

LH: It had to be staged.

JS: What made you know it had to be staged?

LH: Well, because it just came out that way. The first voice that I heard, that came right to me, was Savage Indian. I have to say that this is standard working process with me because I never would have written a baseball novel because I don't know anything about baseball. I still know very little about baseball, and my son is humiliated by that. He says, "Don't tell people that." But it's true. I also didn't know anything about Mary Todd Lincoln. I would never write about her, never, because I didn't like Lincoln, and what he did to the thirty-eight Dakota is a horrific event in US history. The Savage Indian voice came, and then Mary starts telling her story, so I had to tell it. But it came out in this prose poetry style. It's more of a stylized language, and I realized, "Oh, this is poetry, but it's for the stage." It has to be, and I kind of saw it that way. When Mary and Savage Indian have the fighting scene, and she stabs him, I saw it happen on stage. And I heard her voice, so it had to be this way. And I knew I couldn't write a traditional book—you know, it's not a traditional novel per se. Coffee House Press has marketed it as a kind of novel although they don't say it directly. Editor Chris Fischbach has said, "Oh, yes. This is a novel." [*Laughs*] Okay. But it's also poetry for the stage. It lives on stage or is meant to. But maybe his instincts are spot on:

this story lives on the page. And the public have kind of ignored it. Well, maybe not ignored it, considering the reviews and the places it has been staged. And I do know people who are teaching it. *Savage Conversations* has reached an audience, but it's also stylized poetry because people don't talk like that even in the nineteenth century.

JS: Right.

LH: It works for me, and the story came out that way. I thought for the longest time that I was just writing a series of poems, and then it became really visual to me, which is on stage. Then it became a book. I like it. The book makes me happy. [*Laughs*]

JS: Yeah, I would love to stage it myself.

LH: Please do!

JS: I hope to, I hope to! I think I just have one other thing I wanted to quote back to you. I know that you have read this essay written by Sarah Fawn Montgomery for the Poetry Foundation about *Savage Conversations*.[7]

LH: Yeah.

JS: I think I recall you tweeting it, in which she calls the Rope a Greek chorus.

LH: That's right, yes.

JS: I wanted to ask you what you thought of that.

LH: I'm really flattered. I like that a lot. Although I have to say the truth of the Rope. Have I already said this? The Rope came to me in Las Vegas, Nevada, when I was in my hotel bathroom. I've told this story. I'm in the bathroom thinking, getting ready to take a shower. I was in Nevada attending the Western Literature Association Conference, and it was held in Las Vegas that year. I'm getting cleaned up, or I'm gonna get cleaned up, and in floats this noose right through the wall. The noose got about this close to my face [*waves hand in front of face*], and I was kind of shocked. Then he began to talk, and that's how the character's formation came about. What I find most interesting about this is that the noose, the single [actual] noose [used in the hanging of thirty-eight Dakota], was discovered at Fort Snelling in 2014. I was shocked that these two events happened, and I am indirectly a part of that story now.

JS: Right, I think Susan Power mentions that in her introduction? Yeah.

LH: I think she did. So yeah, I told her about the noose floating into the bathroom; I told everybody who would listen. Look, this happened, and it was just meant to be like that. And the Rope is comic relief. You know, at least I think he's pretty funny.

JS: I think he is very funny.

LH: [That comic relief is needed] because it's a harsh story. I didn't like Lincoln; I didn't like Mary Todd Lincoln. I thought they were haughty. I thought it was clear that he hated Indians. "Oh, I'm going to spare the lives of several hundred Natives." Oh, go fuck yourself. The Dakotas didn't do what the government said they did, and you [Lincoln] don't even know if the people you hanged were the perpetrators. Maybe they were, maybe they weren't, but no trial?! Lincoln is this revered person for emancipating African Americans. Yes. But he and his administration really go after American Indians. I think they wanted to make the West free of all Native people. Clear us all out completely. So my book is a kind of "fuck you" to the lies of history.

JS: Yeah. Well, that noose story makes me think of a story that Joy Harjo has told many times about seeing a horse in the backseat of her car. I will tell it to students, and they say, "Okay, so that's magical realism. So she saw a vision." And I say, "No, she says the horse was in the backseat of her car." Not a vision.

LH: Yeah. Not a vision.

JS: But maybe this is a different kind of—magical realism is not the right term—but a different kind of worlds merging, times merging. I mean it's the same thing when you try to talk about how time works, or when times are coexisting in the same place, which obviously happens in *Savage Conversations*, right? It's not that somebody is having a flashback or memory, it's the times coexisting. And now we know that EuroWestern science is confirming that's more how time works, right?

LH: Right, yeah. It bends. We've been trying to say that for millennia.

JS: The people who have been observing natural phenomena for millennia have said that is what we have observed, and told, and passed down.

LH: Exactly.

JS: The other thing it makes me think of is Gwendolyn Brooks saying that she would never look at the same tree as a white person because when she sees a tree, she sees the instrument on which her ancestor could be hung.

LH: That's right. We're looking at very different things happening simultaneously.

JS: Right. There's a double consciousness, maybe, that has a relationship to that remix factor. I mean I think that the way you mix history and archives and media is not dissimilar from the way Black writers like Cornelius Eady, Claudia Rankine, Branden Jacobs-Jenkins use humor and parody and remix to stage an embodied double consciousness.

LH: Yes, I think you're exactly right, and that's how it feels. What we are trying to say is that we are in touch with the marvelous; all of a sudden, those worlds have opened, and you can see the horse in the back seat of the car, and it's not a vision. The horse is in the back seat of the car, and just believe it, and it's there. And the noose is there, and my characters are there. I don't think that we're like a god creating these images; I think we are just seeing what is there. I recognize other artists and other writers of color when they say, "Oh, yes, I see that." I know that they do. Do you know the Copt poet Matthew Shenoda? He's in Chicago right now. He and I were invited to give a reading in Asheville, North Carolina, with poet Allison Hedge Coke, so we decided to go out to the site of Black Mountain College. The three of us all hung out at the site where Buckminster Fuller was teaching, and I saw different things there, and it was just one of these moments. This was a place where all of these poets of the early twentieth century had come to read and teach and just be. We were there, and it moved us all three to just be there. At least, that is the way I remember it. To paraphrase Leslie Silko, "In times like these it happened like this." I don't honestly think we artists are special. But I think that we were taught or learned how to be open.

JS: Right. Double consciousness helps me think about the ways in which people who are not central in the dominant world view, which is most expressed in the world around us, have to develop muscles to translate experience and understanding to match and contrast common representations and the way people around you are saying, "The world is like this," and you say, "Well actually, my experience is not that." We're bumped up against it—like the cultural collision thing—we're bumped up against each other having different experiences. I get so frustrated when dramaturges and critics do try to talk about that as a special essentialist magical Native thing because that's what German Expressionism was trying to say, that we're all capable of experiencing the world in different ways. That's what Brecht was trying to say. I've been writing a lot about Momaday's *The Moon in Two Windows*. And the reviews about that play have been so frustrating because they say, "It's too didactic." There's a scene where a girl who has died has come back as a ghost, and she's putting red spots on her face and on her doll and the other children to tell the story of smallpox. The critics say, "That's so didactic and silly it doesn't match the tragedy of moment and it's"—

LH: Yeah, it does!

JS: They've missed hundreds of years of theatrical tradition in multiple places on the globe. I did want to ask you about ghosts specifically. I'm trying to be careful about how to talk about ghosts in relationship to Native theater because of the stereotype of and romanticization of all of those eighteenth- and nineteenth-century plays in which there's the noble ghost who warns the hero.

LH: Yeah, yeah.

JS: Or the Philip Freneau concept that Native people need to melt away into the landscape, to somehow give honor to the remaining people.

LH: That's crazy, just crazy!

JS: Right, it's crazy, but then I see ghosts coming up again and again in plays of people who were trying to critique those whitestream, colonizing, genocidal cultures. Harvey Young, the theater scholar, talks about the undead in Black theater, which struck me because I had been using the word "unghosting" to talk about ghosts that are resistant, that are refusing to erase or ignore repressed history.

LH: Yeah.

JS: It's not that these writers are trying to give voice to the voiceless because that's an irritating concept, right? That's condescending. Instead, it's a way to point to something that has been there but has been ignored or repressed or erased or buried but has always been present. Right? And that's what settler colonial theory is trying to do, to say this has always been there. We're trying to use language to point to it in order to show the way it works. Harvey Young uses the language of undead to say there's an unstated expectation that, for example, Black characters will die; therefore, there's a marking of death upon them. I'm not sure that's really the most useful way to think about ghosts in Native plays either, but I've been thinking about that so much particularly in *Savage Conversations* and a bit in other pieces where you have ghosts come up. What does that bring up for you, or what are your thoughts on the place of ghosts in these worlds? What is their role? Why do we need them?

LH: Oh, because they're here, they're with us, and so in almost all of my work there are ghosts, whether it's a play or novels. *Savage Conversations* has a ghost who is front and center. The reason that they are so easy for me to write is that we lived with them, and my grandmother would sit up late at night in the house in Ada. I just told John Lowe, a southern literary scholar at UGA, about my grandmother's house, which is now my house in Ada, Oklahoma. I've inherited it from my adopted mom. The front room was where people were laid out when they died. My grandmother's house was where her family would sit up with the dead. When I was really little, probably four or five years old, there was a man who was laid out because they didn't have enough money for a funeral home. He was there, and people would come to visit. I stayed a lot with my grandmother, and one night I got up in the middle of the night, and she said, "Oh, there's old Lum Jones. He just flew down the street and went up through the tree." There's a bird, a blackbird in that vision for her. The next day he was dead. She was talking about her neighbor, and of course he died. She and my great-grandmother and my great-great-great aunt, whom I never met, they were always present in that house. The house was and is filled with ghosts. And ghosts on the front porch. When we remodeled the house, sometimes I would drive up and see my grandfather sitting on the front porch. He's been dead since 1987. I see them, and they are family, and they lived in that house. I see my relatives, and they are always around. Ghosts are very much a part of my life, but they were part of the family legacy. Still with us, always with us. Sometimes ghosts are not family members. When we moved to Cincinnati, there was a man who was a ghost who lived in the house we bought there. Every once in a while, I'd see him out of the corner of my eye, and he smelled like cigar smoke because he was smoking a cigar. I would often smell him before I would see him, and he just lived there in the house. I find it very easy to write about ghosts. I don't have anxieties about ghosts; they're very comforting to me. And I think that "coming together" or collision of the worlds is thin, and that reality is very—undeep—it's thin. Maybe it's romantic, maybe it's a sense of loneliness for my relatives. But I was raised to see ghosts and to not be afraid. I'm writing a new project, a new play, *Unredacted,* for *The Georgia Review.* It should be out in the spring 2020 census issue. I've coauthored it with one of the UGA graduate students because we're doing a big mapping project. The main character is the Lady of Cofitachequi, who was a powerful southeastern Indigenous woman and head of her nation. She meets Hernando de Soto in 1540. Of course, he puts her in chains, and she has to escape. But in our play, she's driving a gold Chrysler DeSoto Adventurer. Um, excuse me: her ride is a gold DeSoto. Gold is what de Soto came looking for in 1540 but could not have.

JS: Of course!

LH: And the Lady of Cofitachequi sings, she dances, and she just—oh, you know, does what she has to do to get her claws into him. Now this is the fun part. You know de Soto dies here in the Southeast. He's gone everywhere, stealing everything, but as he puts one foot in the grave, then the other, *shizam,* he's able to sing a couple of sad songs and then dies. Kind of like an opera. In our version of the play, Coi scratches him, because the name Cofitachequi means star panther. Coi, or Koi, is panther, the "i" is collapsed. Fichik is star. So Cofitachequi is the town name and the mantle of Star

Panther Woman, because it is a woman that shows up to meet de Soto. She wears the trappings of a star panther and is described as being carried on a litter, never touching the ground as she arrives to treat with de Soto. She's very young, and in the documents the litter is described as covered in the skins of animals. She's likely the earthly representation of the dark star in the sky, so we can infer she has "medicine." He tries to get her into his bed, and as a result the plant medicine that she scratches him with, as Star Panther Woman, kills him. Alas, it doesn't happen fast. So Coi and de Soto have time to sing and dance their way to the tragic end of the play.

JS: Oh, good.

LH: And it's meant to be funny. But it's history, and the history of Georgia can be funny. The Star Panther Woman was from Cofitachequi town when they met. It's here in Georgia. He goes on, and she does the medicine thing and then sings her way triumphantly off stage. [*Laughs*] We developed the play this year at UGA. Nathan Bradford Dixon and I are the coauthors. We did a lot of research to piece this history together, and then there's a timeline that he built. There's a lot of artwork with the Lady of Cofitachequi. We'll see how it goes; perhaps next year we'll get a chance at a staged reading.

JS: Oh, that's phenomenal. Yes, I love it! Well, we've talked a little bit about ghosts and memorial and commemoration, which is something that the United States is obsessed with right now. But I also have to talk to you about how the United States is obsessed with Oklahoma right now. I think since I came to your work by looking through Oklahoma settings, I have to ask you some things about Oklahoma.

LH: Okay, sure! You know, I'm writing a collection of poetry and essays with Dean Rader, and we have done two big essays for other things that we have cobbled together for this collection on Oklahoma. We each write a poem about Oklahoma as we create this collection of poems about Oklahoma. We are trying to get at what makes Oklahoma Oklahoma. I'm not sure, and I would say that he's not sure either, that we've actually nailed it yet—what makes Oklahoma Oklahoma. It's because our state is the Frankenstein of states. It was cobbled together in a really ugly way, and then people were cobbled together. Nation-state voiceover: "You're gonna live here even if it kills you, and we hope it does kill you." American Indian voiceover: "We're not gonna die, so eat it." African American voiceover: "Wait a minute, we're not down for this shit, either." And then there's all the hangings of African Americans that go on, and all the land grabs that go on, and then comes the Dust Bowl, and all the races have to hold onto one another to survive. The history of our state is completely fucked up either by God's wrath or human folly or both, all at once. Frankly, I'm surprised I can think at all. Dean and I are trying to create a book of poems about Oklahoma. Meanwhile, Nate Dixon and I are trying to create a play about the Southeast and de Soto and his fool wreckage. Hopefully, both these projects will be finished this year. We'll see.

JS: Oh, great.

LH: We got these crazy names. Oklahoma is a name that comes from two Choctaw words: *Okla* means people, *huma* or *homa* means red. Dean's got several crazy names for our book, so that's right in line with our history.

JS: Well, I am also trying to figure out what makes Oklahoma Oklahoma, and I haven't figured it out either.

LH: It's almost impossible. What makes Oklahoma Oklahoma? I don't know. Um, is it the song? Is it the land rush? No. Is it the thievery? Is it all the love that the people show in a crisis? Yes, it's that, too.

JS: Yeah, well those things are a part of it somehow though. This is a large part of the book proposal I'm working on for Oklahoma poets and playwrights. I recently watched the new *Watchmen* TV series. I don't know if you have heard about it, but it's set in Tulsa, and the 1921 Greenwood Massacre is a huge part of its backstory.

LH: Is it on Netflix?

JS: HBO.

LH: And it's called *Watchmen*?

JS: Yes, it's inspired by the graphic novel *Watchmen* from the 1980s. But it is set in 2019 in Tulsa, and it really missed the opportunity to talk about Indigenous history and Indigenous people. I think partially because they filmed in Atlanta, so nobody was around to say, "Hello."

LH: Georgia doesn't look like Oklahoma.

JS: No, and it's not just Black and white here.

LH: [*Laughs*] It's always that way: anything about Oklahoma misses the fact that there are Indians living here at all.

JS: Yes, although I am enthralled that there are so many projects filming in and around Tulsa and Stillwater right now.

LH: That's great.

JS: Yeah, I was living in Tulsa last year in a house with a ghost who smokes cigarettes.

LH: [*Laughs*] So what were you going to ask me about Oklahoma?

JS: There are some references to the musical *Oklahoma!* in *Watchmen* [which features an all-Black production of the musical]. Between that and the Oregon Shakespeare Festival did a same sex-marriage/gender-flipped

Oklahoma! production a while ago, there's a lot of work coming up for the anniversary of the musical, and then there's a production on Broadway that's supposed to show a dark side of the musical. If they had read Lynn Riggs's play [*Green Grow the Lilacs* from 1931 on which the musical was based], they would have known that!

LH: [*Laughs*]

JS: First of all, it's not white.[8] And, second of all, it's not picnics and roses.

LH: Yeah, yeah, yeah.

JS: I just see Oklahoma popping up in pop culture in such mysterious ways, and I kept thinking it's not surprising to me because it is a place of cultural collision, and then I heard Rilla Askew—she writes in *Most American: Notes from a Wounded Place*—say it's a microcosm of North America. Of course, all of the weirdness is all compacted into this place.

LH: It is, and Rilla is exactly right.

JS: Yeah.

LH: But it's something more, that I'm not sure any of us have been able to define. I think that the song and the musical and Lynn Riggs's original work have even made it harder to define —because Riggs couldn't define it.

JS: Right.

LH: It's also the thing that kills you: why is Oklahoma written about by people who no longer live there?

JS: Right.

LH: We have been trying to tackle that in our poetry book because neither one of us lives there, may not be able to live there again. I don't know. I keep trying to return, and it's the site of return for me, but I may not live there in the end although it's the place I know best.

JS: Right, and there are these ways in which Oklahoma reaches out into the world and is imbricated in international events. I know that you and Choctaw historian Jacki Rand did some work thinking about the Irish memorials to Choctaw donations and other nations' donations during the potato famine, right?

LH: Right. *Famine Pots: The Choctaw-Irish Gift Exchange, 1847–Present*, with prefaces by the president of Ireland, Michael Higgins, and Gary Batton, chief of the Choctaw Nation, will be out in September 2020. This is a book coedited by Irish scholar Padraig Kirwan and me. We have worked on the book for several years. In fact, that's what I've been doing all week is editing the essays. There are four Irish and four Choctaw scholars. Of the Choctaws, Jacki Rand is one, Phil Morgan is another, Tim Tingle, and me.

JS: Oh, that's great.

LH: It's already been copyedited, and it will be out for the fall 2020. We have all these images. I just went to Ireland in May to look at the National Famine Museum, in Strokestown, and then I gave a talk at the museum while I was there. We will do a book launch in Georgia, and then we will go to Ireland for a book launch. It's a history in 1847 in which the Choctaws find out there is a famine in Ireland, and they say, "Oh, that's terrible, they're starving to death." So the Choctaws take up a collection at Doaksville, Indian Territory, and send the money to Ireland.

JS: Right.

LH: That's because Oklahoma Indians certainly had to erase boundaries due to all the tribes being squeezed into one place. It's crazy making. Of course, they did have tribal boundaries in 1847. But the point is Natives have always been generous when people are in need. And then we have a governor like Mary Fallon who tried to relegate us into nonexistence again. Meanwhile her damn kid parked a trailer house on the lawn of the governor's mansion. You know, she did that.

JS: Yeah, and she was wearing a pink feathered headdress.

LH: I know, I know. Damn it, why do they all have to wear faux headdresses? There's a reason that American Indians just go stark raving mad. Look at what we have to contend with!

JS: Right, but what you say about the boundaries is interesting because no wonder Oklahomans don't recognize boundaries. . . . All over the continent, there's a whole string of treaties where they said, "These are the boundaries forever," then later, "Oh, just kidding, *these* are the boundaries forever," then later, "Oh, just kidding, wait. *These—*"

LH: "These are the boundaries." It's almost as if it was a poem actually. And what happens is that boundaries are a trash compactor.

JS: [*Laughs*]

LH: That's exactly what Oklahoma is, and it's killing us. I talk to the Okies all the time. You know, Rilla Askew is really brave, and she only recently moved home and had to confront some of that stuff, and Phil Morgan lives at home, and another friend who is a poet, scholar, is Ken Hada, he lives in Oklahoma, but sometimes the culture and history wears thin. At other times, I'm so proud of all of us.

JS: Yeah.

LH: It's very hard for artists to confront our past and live with it in ways that don't eat you up. Now you've got the cowboy poets and that whole gang of folks that go out to Guthrie every year, and they love it. And I'm glad they have those things. But for some of us, no. It's hard, it's very hard.

JS: Mary Kathryn Nagle and I have been talking about that: we keep leaving, and then missing it, so we go back and leave again. Going, wait, why are we here? Yeah.

LH: I keep doing the same thing. I'll go home, I'll get a leave of absence, and I'll go home and stay. And we fix up the house, it's so cute, and then we leave, because after a while it's like, okay, y'all are killing me. [*Laughs*]

JS: Yeah, but in that trash compactor, inside, in the process of breaking down and regenerating, there are little fires building. There's always something new coming out of it.

LH: It'll blow up one of these days.

JS: It will; it will blow up one way or the other. Okay, well, so with Mary Kathryn's advice and inspired by her hashtag with Larissa FastHorse, the "Instead of Redface" hashtag, I'm working on an online resource for Native theater.

LH: That's so awesome!

JS: That's an ongoing project that I've been doing relationship-building for, so every time I get to talk to a playwright or a theater artist, I ask, "What would you want to be on such a thing? What would you hope, what would be useful for audiences and producers and other theater folks on such an online resource?"

LH: I think an online resource that targets towns or is town-centric. Because many of us who are Oklahomans, as you know, write out of certain towns. Not the big towns necessarily, but I would say "yes" for Tulsa, for Oklahoma City, but Blackwell, Bartlesville, Bug Tussle. With this online resource, you're talking about theater in Oklahoma?

JS: I'm talking about theater in Oklahoma, but also more broadly Native theater. I think the situation north of the Great Lakes in Canada has been that there are many more resources and many more productions and many more publications, so I am looking primarily within US boundaries. I'm wanting to create something that will help promote the plays, basically. Different people have had different ideas. Nobody wants to be gatekeeping to say, "This is what Native theater is." Right, nobody wants that. Diane Glancy said, "I'll give you all my plays, and you can just put them online," and I thought, "That's great, but lots of people are not going to want to do that." So that's not the answer. Rhiana Yazzie from New Native Theatre said, "If you want to be useful, make something that will get audiences ready for our work because non-Native audiences are not ready for these plays." They don't respond to them in useful or productive ways, so think about audiences, right? And then other authors say, "Well, I just want to help producers making theater find me."

LH: I think towns. Why don't Oklahoma writers have a different kind of footprint? Because if you say you're from Oklahoma, you're dismissed because there are no towns. No LA, no NYC. Oklahoma has a lack of town identity, and town identity is the basis of tribalism, especially among the Five Tribes. It was the town that defined you. In some ways, the work that I do is set in towns in Oklahoma for that reason, and I think that helps people get to know us in ways that are surprising. That's just what I would suggest. So much of my work is from McAlester or Ada, and right now I'm writing this new novel set in Allen and in Beirut in Bilaad ash Sham. Allen is a border town between old Choctaws and more out west towns, you know, a border town between tribes. It always was, and it's where the peanut farms were back in the day. I'm interested in that town culture, so maybe that's why I'm saying it. I think towns have a very important role for Indians and non-Indians in the making of Oklahoma.

JS: Great, I'm going to take you up on that.

LH: Okay.

JS: Well, towns perform.

LH: That's right.

JS: The other thing that I wanted to ask you about is the embodiment of mounds, and so are towns scripts in the same way that mounds are?

LH: Yes. I just came back from Mobile, Alabama, and the Mabila Indians are Choctawan or part of our Confederacy of Choctawan towns. The first thing you read in the historical record about Mabila Indians and Mobilians was that Mabila was a trade language between Indians and the French. It's our earliest trade language with the French. We have one historical document in which it was written out. This is from 1702 or 1708, something like that. I was just down there, and the mounds are around there. Also, Ocmulgee town has these huge giant mounds! All of the ancient towns, like Tuscaloosa, for example, have a mound within them or around them. The answer is yes. These mound towns in the 1700s represented a group of people, and the earthworks also represented the town and the people. I am going out to Seattle because I've been working with Chadwick Allen for many years. He's the associate provost at the University of Washington. I'm also going to give a talk about mounds and mound complexes while I'm there. Then the theater department is doing a reading of *Savage Conversations*. I'll be out there on January 20, 2020. Nevertheless, this is the most important aspect of Oklahoma culture. Town mounds, I mean. When we think of mound towns, we think of Spiro. There's a mound there. Used to be mounds all over, and still with all the plowing, there's still mounds. There are mounds outside of Ada, outside of Maude, and they were just the way of scripting the land for future generations. A mound has a character, just like a town. It has a script about itself, and it performs with the earth's revolving around the sun. Oh! And we didn't even talk about my friend Monique Mojica—my work with Monique and our play, *Sideshow Freaks and Circus Injuns*. Monique is so talented. She's an amazing actor, playwright, and scholar.

JS: Yes.

LH: [Monique and I] finished that first draft, and we had a reading performance. We need to mount the play. We took four years to go all over the country and map these mounds and then map them onto our bodies and then perform them.

JS: Well, next time. We'll talk about that next time.

LH: Next time.

Notes

1. Jodi A. Byrd, *The Transit of Empire: Indigenous Critiques of Colonialism* (University of New Mexico Press, 2011), p. 20. All notes with this interview are by the editor of this volume. All ellipses in the interview indicate text omitted by the editor. Bracketed content insertions in the interview were made by the editor for this volume.

2. Associate professor in the School of Theatre and Dance and a core faculty member in Women's and Gender Studies at Illinois State University.

3. Shook is referring to a videopoem by LeAnne Howe and director R. Vincent Moniz Jr., with artwork and animation by Jonathan Thunder.

4. "Advice to Myself 2: Resistance." Directed by Heid E. Erdrich, written and performed by Louise Erdrich, filmed and edited by Elizabeth Day, music by Trevino Brings Plenty. https://vimeo.com/127847220.

5. Nathan Scott McNamara, "Eyes Cracking like Egg Yolks: LeAnne Howe's 'Savage Conversations,'" *Los Angeles Review of Books*, 20 February 2019, https://lareviewofbooks .org/article/eyes-cracking-like-egg-yolks-leanne-howes-savage-conversations/.

6. Annette Lapointe, Review of *Savage Conversations*, *New York Journal of Books*, https://www.nyjournalofbooks.com/book-review/savage-conversations.

7. Sarah Fawn Montgomery, "Native Ghosts: Genocide and Madness Collide in a Reinterpretation of Mary Todd Lincoln," *Poetry Foundation*, 18 February 2019, https:// www.poetryfoundation.org/articles/149201/native-ghosts.

8. Rollie Lynn Riggs was Cherokee, and the play was set in Indian Territory.

Index

Abenaki people, 55

academic writing: activism and, 94–96; novels contrasted with, 4; recovery of history via, 24; story as motivating, 65; time and space as changed through, 24. *See also* research by LH

activism: in *Miko Kings*, 23; in *Shell Shaker*, 94; writing and, 94–96

Ada, Oklahoma, 104–5, 120, 143–44, 150–51

adoption by American Indians: fictive kinship, 100; of LH, xiv, xvii, 62, 97–101, 103, 104–5; of non-Indians, 55; taking in runaway enslaved people, 17, 26, 33

African American–Native American connections: Choctaws as taking in enslaved runaways, 17, 26, 33; as defying models of race and racism, 33; first collaboration in Texas between, xviii; intermarriage, 16–17, 26; in *Miko Kings*, xi, 7, 16–17, 66; musical roots, 33; overview, 32–33. *See also* Hampton University (previously Hampton Normal School for Blacks and Indians)

African Americans: Black literature, and embodied double consciousness, 141; Black theater, the

"undead" in, 143, 146; blamed as "Other" for white women's insanity, 92; civil rights movement, 47; white supremacist violence in Oklahoma/Indian Territory, 17, 145, 146. *See also* African American–Native American connections; Black/white binary and erasure of Indigenous peoples; enslaved persons; racial divide

agriculture, 32, 71

Alaska, 130

Allen, Chadwick, 49, 53n12, 84, 107, 127, 128, 150; *Trans-Indigenous: Methodologies for Global Literary Studies*, 34

Allen, Oklahoma, 150

Allen, Paula Gunn, 132; *Spider Woman's Granddaughters*, 113n1

Allotment Act, *Miko Kings* used to teach about, 66

American Indian Returnings (lecture series), 107–8

American Indians. *See* Native Americans/American Indians

"American in New York, An" (short story), 113n1

American mainstream. *See* mainstream culture; southern culture, Native cultures informing

About the Editor

Kirstin L. Squint is the author of *LeAnne Howe at the Intersections of Southern and Native American Literature* (LSU Press, 2018), a coeditor of *Swamp Souths: Literary and Cultural Ecologies* (LSU Press, 2020), and a contributor to *Appalachian Reckoning: A Region Responds to "Hillbilly Elegy"* (West Virginia University Press, 2019), winner of the 2020 American Book Award for criticism. She holds the Whichard Visiting Distinguished Professorship in the Humanities at East Carolina University (2019–2022).